Birmingham Hidden Walks

Robert Ankcorn &
Ruby Compton-Davies

To Rob's family for their Birmingham pride, and partner Anna for her love and patience. To Ruby's Mum and Dad for their love and support. To our friends and siblings for treading the streets of Brum for us. To lasting friendship.

Published by Geographers'
A-Z Map Company Limited
An imprint of HarperCollins Publishers
Westerhill Road
Bishopbriggs
Glasgow
G64 2QT

HarperCollins*Publishers*
Macken House, 39/40 Mayor Street Upper, Dublin 1,
D01 C9W8, Ireland

www.az.co.uk
a-z.maps@harpercollins.co.uk

1st edition 2022

Text and routes © Robert Ankcorn
and Ruby Compton-Davies 2022
Mapping © Collins Bartholomew Ltd 2022

This product uses map data licenced from
Ordnance Survey© Crown copyright and
database rights 2021 OS 100018598

A catalogue record for this book
is available from the British Library.

ISBN 978-0-00-849630-2

10 9 8 7 6 5 4 3 2

Printed in India

This book contains FSC™ certified paper and other controlled
sources to ensure responsible forest management.

For more information visit: www.harpercollins.co.uk/green

contents

introduction

Birmingham. Once the 'Workshop of the World'. Once much maligned in popular culture. But always possessing an independent swagger, a self-deprecating sense of humour and a disregard for history with the city's motto 'Forward'. This book will help you discover the hidden history and lost gems that deserve to be more widely known. A consistent feature of these walks is the examples of civic pride expressed through the sculptures by Bloye and Creswick, the decorative pubs by James & Lister Lea and the aspirational schoolhouses by Martin & Chamberlain. Another obvious thread is the monumental ambition of the city's postwar reconstruction with the increasingly rare brutalist architecture featuring in many routes.

There is no denying that Birmingham still, too often, feels built for the automobile. These walks therefore often unfold along canals, under junctions and through green walkways in order to discover the City's distinct areas. Exploring Birmingham by foot is radical and enjoyable. Hopefully it will become easier in the future too.

We guarantee this book will take you to parts of the city you haven't been before. It's also very likely that the lesser-trodden routes will become your favourites. Every part of the city has its own captivating story and we hope you enjoy exploring them as much as we do.

about the authors

Robert Ankcorn grew up in Birmingham and his passion for its history and folklore emerged from exploring by bike as a teenager, while Ruby Compton-Davies is a proud adoptee of the city and believes the buzz of Brum is something everybody should appreciate. In 2016 Rob and Ruby co-founded the walking tour company, Real Birmingham, and have since delighted thousands of guests with their tales of the UK's second city. When they aren't touring around their beloved Birmingham, Ruby is a full-time English teacher and passionate activist. Rob is Operations Manager at an NHS hospital, plays in a ukulele band, and says he is a newly suffering supporter of Birmingham City FC.

how to use this book

Each of the 20 walks in this guide is set out in a similar way.
They are all introduced with a brief description, including notes on things you will encounter on your walk, and a photograph of a place of interest you might pass along the way.

On the first page of each walk there is a panel of information outlining the distance of the walk, a guide to the walking time, and a brief description of the path conditions

or the terrain you will encounter. A suggested starting point along with the nearest postcode is shown, although postcodes can cover a large area therefore this is just a rough guide.

The major part of each section is taken up with route maps and detailed point-to-point directions for the walk. The route instructions are prefixed by a number in a circle, and the corresponding location is shown on the map.

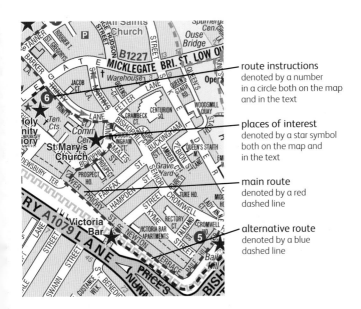

route instructions
denoted by a number in a circle both on the map and in the text

places of interest
denoted by a star symbol both on the map and in the text

main route
denoted by a red dashed line

alternative route
denoted by a blue dashed line

A̅Z̅ walk one

City Squares

Architecture, politics and canals.

The small settlement of Bermingeham acquired a market charter in 1166 and grew to be Britain's second city without any natural advantage other than its location. Next to the foundries and mines of the Black Country and sitting in the centre of England, it thrived as a commercial and iron merchant hub from the 16th century onwards. The city centre is a jungle of diverse architectural styles punctuated by the Second World War marks of the luftwaffe and carved up by 1960s highways. This contrast makes exploring the city uniquely intriguing. What's more, it is constantly changing. There's an old saying, 'Birmingham will be great when it's finished'... This has been said for a hundred years!

This walk starts at St Philips Cathedral, which was built in 1715 after St Martin's Church could no longer accommodate the growing town. Originally consecrated as a parish church and later becoming the city's Anglican cathedral in 1905, it is the third smallest cathedral in England and a fine example of English Baroque architecture. As you walk, you will discover the mystery of the cathedral's 33-inch grave, the secret pawprint at Queen Victoria's feet and how two buildings tell the tale of Jewish emancipation in the UK.

This walk can be combined with walk 2 to create a circular tour of the city centre.

start	St Philips Cathedral, Colmore Row
nearest postcode	B3 2QB
finish	The Mailbox, Royal Mail Street
distance	1½ miles / 2.4 km
	(4 miles / 6.4 km if combined with walk 2)
time	45 minutes
	(1 hour 45 minutes if combined with walk 2)
terrain	Pavements and paved paths, some steps.

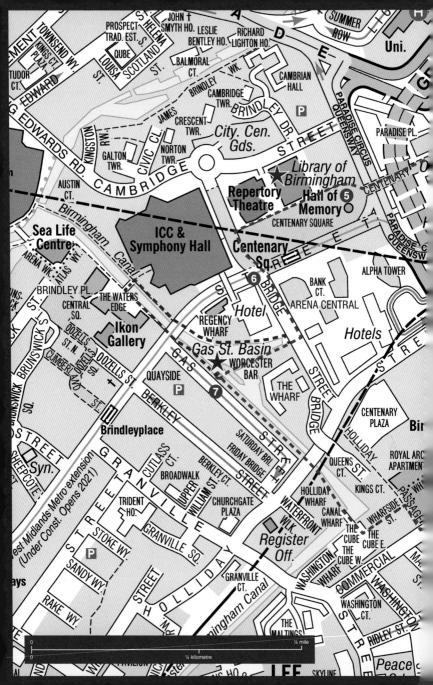

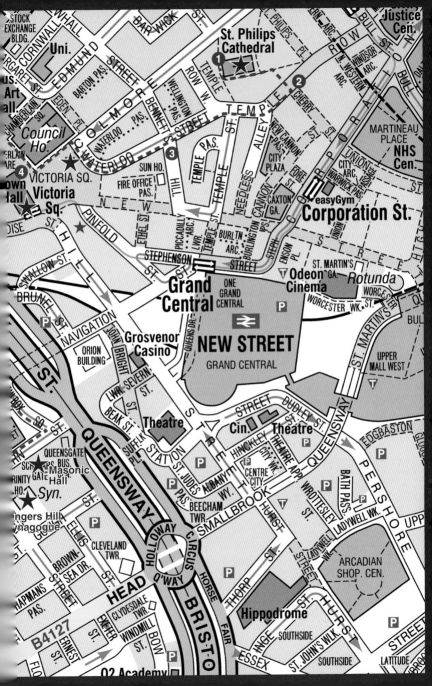

1 Start at the front of St Philips Cathedral ★ . Facing the right corner of the cathedral, you will see a tiny grave. This is the resting place of Nanette Stocker, who toured the country as 'the smallest woman in the kingdom' and died in 1819 whilst in the city to perform. She was just 33 inches (84 centimetres) tall. As you face the front of the cathedral, continue down the right side of the building. Pass the Burnaby Memorial obelisk and take the next path on the right. At the end of this path, on the left, there is a memorial to two construction workers who died building the Town Hall. Fittingly, the memorial is a fluted column identical to the ones on the Town Hall itself.

2 Turn right onto Temple Row and pass Needless Alley, which was famous in the early 1800s as a street of ill repute. ('Needless by name and needless by nature' wrote the *Birmingham Journal*.) Continue as far as Waterloo Street, turn left here and walk to the junction with Bennett's Hill. Look inside the porch of the far left's National Provincial Bank (1870). The four relief panels tell the tale of Birmingham's industries: metalworking, glassblowing, electroplating and gunmaking.

3 Stay on Waterloo Street to reach Victoria Square ★ , where the monarch's statue has pride of place despite the rumour that she supposedly rolled down the blinds in her royal train carriage to avoid looking at the city! At her feet is a paving slab marked with a pawprint commemorating Ebony, a black labrador owned by one of the construction workers who remodelled the square in 1993. She is said to have carried tools for her master.

4 Exit the square at the far right corner, which leads into Chamberlain Square. On your left is the Town Hall (1844) ★ which was built in a classical Roman style and resembles a temple. Here in 1901, David Lloyd George had to be disguised as a policeman and smuggled out of a side door to escape a riot caused by his rally against the Boer War. The war was led principally by the square's dedicatee, former city mayor Joe Chamberlain, who changed the city more than any other. The Chamberlain Memorial Fountain (1880) commemorates his work. Look out for Thomas Attwood reclining on the steps near the west corner of the Town Hall. He is admiring the building he helped commission before winning electoral representation for cities with the Birmingham Political Union. Opposite the clock tower colloquially known as 'Big Brum' is Centenary Way, which sits in between the recently remodelled buildings of the Paradise development. Follow this into Centenary Square.

5 Walk around the right of the Hall of Memory (1925) – the female statue commemorates the Women's Services. On your right is Baskerville House, a civic building on the former site of famous printer John Baskerville's home. A radical enlightenment atheist figure, his body has been reburied twice and put on display once. It remains in Warstone Cemetery contrary to his wishes not to be buried in consecrated grounds. Next to this is the Library of Birmingham ★ , opened in 2013. Go to level 7's viewing platform 'The Secret Garden' to see Perrott's Folly, which inspired the city's most famous author, J. R. R. Tolkien. On level 9 is the intricately wood-panelled Shakespeare Memorial Room. This was originally built in the City's Victorian Library (1882) and, saved from the demolition, was rebuilt atop the library encased in a golden rotunda. Exit the library and cross over the road directly in front of you on the other side of the square, using the pedestrian crossing along the road to the right.

6 Turn and walk down Bridge Street. Take the first footpath on the right into Gas Street Basin ★ , which is arguably the most important spot in the country's canal network. Walk along Worcester Bar, which once provided a physical barrier between the two rival canal companies. An Act of Parliament forced the two canals to join up in the early 19th century. Take the footbridge over the canal, turn right down the brick path and turn right on the canal.

(The footbridge was closed during the Covid-19 pandemic. If this is still the case, retrace your steps and take the footpath that was on your right as you exited Bridge Street. Walk under the tunnel, over the footbridge outside the ICC and back under the tunnel.)

7 Walk along the canal and over 'Lover's Bridge' where couples confident in their eternal love can attach an engraved padlock and cast the key into the canal. Follow the canal around to the left and turn right before The Mailbox. Walk down the passageway and turn left along Commercial Street.

8 At the end of Commercial Street, two buildings tell a tale. Turn right on Blucher Street and take a few steps to admire Singers Hill Synagogue (1856) ★ on the left. It is one of the oldest 'Cathedral Synagogues' in the country, with grand architecture such as the rose window reflecting the era of Jewish emancipation in the 19th century. Now turn back on yourself and turn right down Severn Street. The terraced building at number 60 was the original synagogue that Singers Hill replaced and is now the Masonic Hall ★ . Note the much more unassuming architecture. Walk to the end of the road and turn left to finish at the entrance to The Mailbox shopping centre ★ .

A꡶Z walk two

Commerce and Culture

Hidden murals and heavy metal in the city centre.

Despite being compact, Birmingham's city centre is full of hidden gems. This walk turns to the bustling streets that have been the focus of commercial life in the city for centuries. Whilst Birmingham was once the home of brutalist architecture, examples of this are now becoming increasingly difficult to find. In addition to the Signal Box and the endangered modernist Corporation Square, you will see the hidden concrete mural saved from the demolition of the original 1960s Bull Ring shopping centre.

You will discover a pub with a grizzly tale, the birthplace of heavy metal and the site of the most infamous speech in British history. Finishing up in the Colmore conservation area, you will see the epicentre of the Arts and Crafts movement – the School of Art – whose students and teachers left their mark all over the city. This is the lesser-known side of Birmingham, summed up by the motto: Through the Gains of Industry we promote Art.

This walk is standalone or can be picked up where walk 1 finished to complete a circular tour of the city centre.

start	The Mailbox, Royal Mail Street
nearest postcode	B1 1RS
finish	St Philips Cathedral, Colmore Row
distance	2½ miles / 4 km
	(4 miles / 6.4 km if combined with walk 1)
time	1 hour (1 hour 45 minutes if combined with walk 1)
terrain	Pavements, paved walkways and steps.

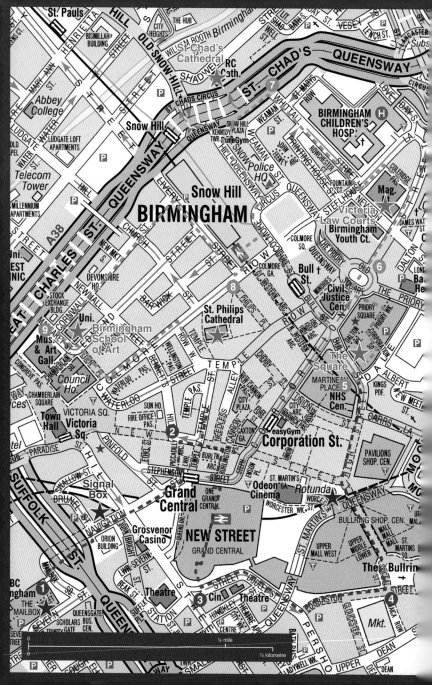

1 Begin outside The Mailbox shopping centre ★. Walk under the A38 in front of you, over the zebra crossing and onto Navigation Street. On your left is the uncompromising New Street Station Signal Box (1964) ★. Grade II listed, this could well become the city's lasting example of its brutalist postwar reconstruction. At the end of Navigation Street, cross over Stephenson Street at the pedestrian crossing and go straight into Piccadilly Arcade. Built in 1910 as a picture house, it was converted into an attractive indoor shopping street just sixteen years later. Look up at the ceiling as you walk through the arcade for a brilliant Renaissance-style secret mural by Paul Maxfield (1989).

2 Exit the arcade and turn right along New Street. Briefly walk up Temple Street on your next left to see the sumptuous 1902 frontage of The Trocadero. A former landlord, Henry Skinner, was shot dead here in a row over wages and is still said to haunt the pub. Retrace your steps and resume walking along New Street, taking the next right into Burlington Arcade. The hotel above was where Wolverhampton MP Enoch Powell made his infamous 'Rivers of Blood' speech in 1968. Exit the arcade at the other end, cross over the road and enter Birmingham New Street Station via the entrance directly opposite Burlington Arcade. Walk through, parallel to the platform screens and out of the Southside Exit.

3 Walk down the steps to see the birthplace of heavy metal: The Crown. This was where the four original stars of Black Sabbath played their first gig together in 1968. Now in a sorry state, there is a campaign to save the pub, with some saying it should reopen as a heavy metal-themed boutique hotel! Turn left down Station Street and past The Electric Cinema (1909), which is the oldest working cinema in the country. In the 1970s it showed 'adult' films but is now restored to its former glory with an art deco frontage. Continue down Dudley Street under Smallbrook Queensway. Before turning left onto Edgbaston Street, on your right you may find street art by brilliant local artist Annatomix, who has curated this space since 2016. Walk down Edgbaston Street with the Fish Market and Rag Market on your right.

4 Turn left in front of St Martin's Church. Whilst most of this church was built in 1873, there has been a church on this site since 1290. Walk past the spire with the outdoor 'Miller's Pulpit', the only one of its kind in the country. Take the steps to the left of the Bullring entrance and walk up the slope. Underneath the iconic cylindrical Rotunda (1965) ★ on the left, the intrepid explorer can discover a mural largely hidden from view. In the first shop that you come to directly beneath the building, on the first floor, is a section of John Poole's impressive concrete mural *The Rotunda Relief* which was saved during the Bullring redevelopment. Bear right and walk to the end of High Street.

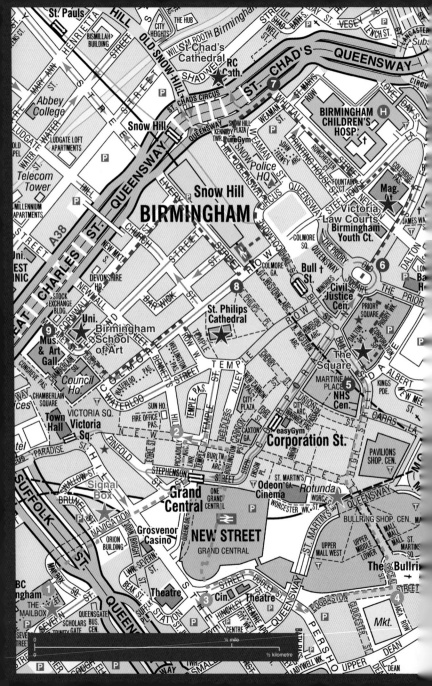

5 Cross over Bull Street and enter Corporation Square (1966) – now called The Square shopping centre ★ – on the right. Designed by Frederick Gibberd of Liverpool Metropolitan Cathedral fame, the understated modernist centre has been host to counter-cultural hub 'Oasis Market' for over fifty years. Walk through the square with the clock tower and take the far left passage. Turn left on exit, cross Corporation Street and then cross over Old Square past the Tony Hancock memorial. Continue onto Corporation Street.

6 This is one of the best-preserved stretches in the city. Walk down the street and past the terracotta Victoria Law Courts (1891) ★ on your left. Queen Victoria herself is seated like a judge above the main entrance, with St George slaying the dragon immediately beneath. Turn left into Coleridge Passage. At the end of this, turn left onto Steelhouse Lane and look out for the city's motto – 'Forward' – above a back entrance to the Law Courts. Turn right onto Whittall Street and walk its length.

7 Turn left onto Queensway to see Pugin's Gothic revival St Chad's Cathedral (1841) ★ from across the road. This was the first Catholic cathedral built in England since the reformation. This area was known for gun manufacturing, which made it a target during the Second World War. In November 1940, an incendiary bomb

crashed through the roof, bounced off the floor and hit some central heating pipes which burst, saving the cathedral from destruction. Take the next left up Snow Hill Queensway. At the end, cross over and turn right into Colmore Circus Queensway. Carefully cross the tram lines and walk up the steps onto the square outside Snow Hill Station. Cross the square and turn right into Colmore Row.

8 Take the next right to understand the meaning behind the old local saying 'a face as long as Livery Street'. At the corner of Edmund Street is a pub named in dedication to the ex-servicemen that drank there and who proudly revelled in Kaiser Wilhelm's dismissive label of 'contemptible little army' regarding the First World War British Expeditionary Force. On the right opposite Cornwall Street, an arched entrance of the old Snow Hill Station survives complete with Great Western Railway logos. Turn left onto Cornwall Street and walk all the way to the end, through the heart of the Colmore conservation area.

9 At the end of Cornwall Street, on the left, is the Ruskin-inspired masterpiece, the Birmingham School of Art (1985) ★ . Check out the rose window of carved foliage around the corner. Continue along Margaret Street then turn left and walk through the pedestrianized Eden Place. At the end, turn left down Colmore Row to finish at St Philips Cathedral ★ .

◮ walk three

Diamonds, Coffins and Clocks

The Jewellery Quarter.

You won't find many more hidden gems than in Birmingham's very own Jewellery Quarter! The district is widely regarded as the birthplace of the city's industry, helping to establish Birmingham as the 'City of a Thousand Trades'. As the Industrial Revolution took over Birmingham and beyond, by 1880 there were over 700 jewellery workshops in this area. Today, the Jewellery Quarter contains Europe's largest concentration of jewellery manufacturers and produces 40 per cent of the UK's jewellery output.

This almost circular walk will showcase some of the history and heritage of the quarter. An apt symbol of its heritage can be found in the distinctive letterboxes that were forged in the Georgian era, with their unique arched design and detail. They were primarily installed to provide a secure drop-off point for precious stones and metals during the 1800s, but over 200 years later they remain, some still in use.. There are twenty-one to spot on your walk, set into the walls of some of the old buildings.

Another focal point of the Jewellery Quarter that offers an insight to the past is its two cemeteries: Warstone Lane and Key Hill. The prodigious number of notable figures laid to rest here illustrates the significance of the Jewellery Quarter to Birmingham's growth, not to mention the wider impact these people had on Britain. Architecturally, the catacombs of Warstone Lane provide a striking backdrop to Birmingham's innovative neighbourhood and its pioneering people.

start	The Queens Arms, Newhall Street
nearest postcode	B3 1RY
finish	St Paul's Square
distance	3½ miles / 5.5 km
time	1 hour 30 minutes
terrain	Pavements and paved paths, some steps.

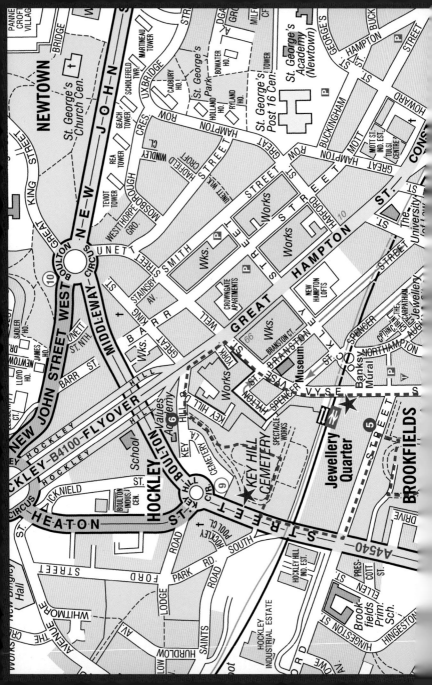

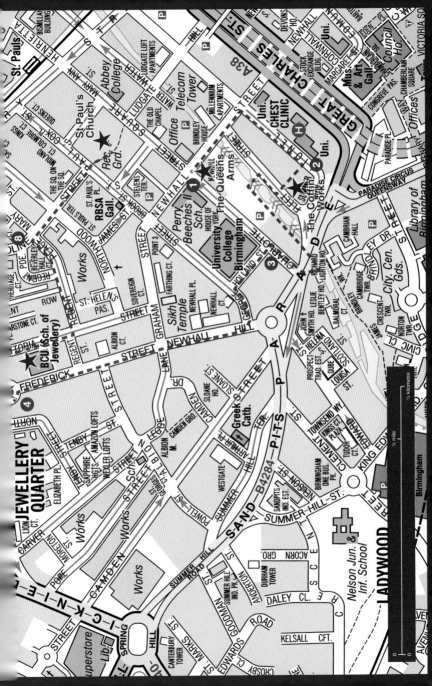

1 Begin this walk at The Queens Arms ★, a stalwart Jewellery Quarter pub. Built in 1870, its nouveau sign attracts punters and TV crews alike, with programmes such as *Line of Duty* having been filmed inside. With the pub on your right, continue down Newhall Street. Take the second right onto Lionel Street. Fun fact: Livery Street, Lionel Street and other streets of the Jewellery Quarter have often been used in film and TV, most notably in Steven Spielberg's *Ready Player One* and the Lloyds Bank famous black horse advert.

2 After a couple of minutes, take the footpath on your right just past the Ibis hotel and continue down the steps to come out onto Fleet Street. Immediately on your left you'll see the Newman Brothers' famous Coffin Works museum ★. Cross over the road and turn right, then cross the canal using the footbridge with the white double archway. Turn left and follow the canal past the locks and under the bridge for the main road. Immediately after the underpass there is access up to the main road on your right and slightly behind you – take this opportunity to exit the canal side. Turn left and carefully cross the dual carriageway using the island in the middle, then turn down Charlotte Street.

3 Take the first left onto Holland Street, which is paved with the typical cobbles of the Jewellery Quarter, and continue to the end. Turn left onto George Street and at the end, turn right onto Newhall Hill. You will go over a set of crossroads where the road turns into Frederick Street, with the Pen Museum on your left. Continue to the top where you will reach the roundabout with a striking green 'Chamberlain Clock' ★. This clock was first unveiled in 1903, to commemorate Joseph Chamberlain's visit to South Africa following the end of the Boer War. Better known for other historical events, Chamberlain's role as Secretary of State for the Colonies and his involvement in the British Empire are the subjects of research by the Jewellery Quarter Heritage team.

4 At the roundabout, turn left onto Warstone Lane and cross over. Continue down Warstone Lane (past the Grade II listed Tibbatts Abel building which used to be an entrance lodge) until you see the gated entrance to Warstone Lane Cemetery ★ (also known as Brookfields Cemetery or Mint Cemetery due to its proximity to the Birmingham Mint). Enter the cemetery and explore all the paths to find some hidden gems. The cemetery was established as a Church of England burial ground in 1847 and some extremely interesting figures are laid to rest here. You'll find innovators such as John Baskerville (pioneer printer), Thomas Henry Gem (co-inventor of lawn tennis) and Lincoln Jefferies (inventor of the Lincoln Air Rifle). You can also try and find the gravestones of people of notable status or death, for example Edward Warulan (son of an Aboriginal king), William Edward Hipkins (lost in the *Titanic* disaster) and George Snipe (a policeman murdered by a member of the notorious Peaky Blinders gang). Of particular interest, also, may be the two-tiered catacombs that you are able to walk on and around.

5 After walking around the cemetery, exit via the path at the opposite side to where you entered, onto Pitsford Street. Turn left and continue until you meet the main road of Icknield Street, then turn right. Continue along Icknield Street and under the bridge until you can enter Key Hill Cemetery ⭐ through the gated entrance on your right. Another cemetery full of hidden gems, it opened in 1836 as a nondenominational or nonconformist burial site and almost has too many notable or interesting gravestones to look out for! There are 46 war graves here (38 from the First World War and eight from the Second) and it also houses the graves of five former Birmingham mayors. Some trailblazing women are also buried here: Marie Bethel Beauclerc (first woman reporter in England and first female teacher at a public boys' school), Harriet Martineau (influential feminist, journalist and writer), Constance Caroline Naden (philosopher and writer) and Mary Showell Rogers (social reformer and pioneer of Birmingham's first Women's Hospital). Well-known names, including Alfred Bird (inventor of custard powder) and Joseph Chamberlain (politician), are commonplace here and in the company of footballers, activists, soldiers, actors and philanthropists.

6 After exploring Key Hill Cemetery, head towards the exit on the north side that comes out onto Key Hill. Turn right and walk to the end of the road, then turn right onto Hockley Hill. Continue down Hockley Hill and take the first right onto Vyse Street. Follow this road, going straight over the crooked crossroads. Continue down Vyse Street, paying particular attention to the original Banksy mural ⭐ on the black walls near the railway station; when this artwork appeared in December 2019, it physically featured a local homeless man named Ryan whom the artist filmed for his short video, *God Bless Birmingham*. Continue past the railway station along Vyse Street until you meet the roundabout and the 'Chamberlain Clock' once again. Turn left at the clock onto Warstone Lane and use the pelican crossing to cross over, then continue down the road.

7 Take the first right onto Vittoria Street. On your right, you will pass the Grade II listed building of the Birmingham School of Jewellery ★, founded in 1890 and the largest jewellery school in Europe. Take the first left onto Regent Place. A local working men's committee presented Charles Dickens with a diamond ring designed and made at a workshop here, in 1852. Dickens loved the people of Birmingham and their industrious yet benevolent attitudes; he said he would replace his own old diamond ring with his 'Birmingham jewel' to remind him of his 'good friends'. As you continue down Regent Place, look up and to the right in order to spy a blue plaque at the former residence of James Watt, the inventor whose steam engine adaptations, arguably, propelled the Industrial Revolution around Britain and the world.

8 At the end of Regent Place, turn right onto Caroline Street and walk to the end, looking out for the spire of St Paul's Church ★ and the BT Tower in the distance ahead. Cross over to access St Paul's Square. In the centre of the square, St Paul's Church has been at the heart of the Jewellery Quarter since 1779 and the square itself remains a hive of activity. This is a lovely area to stop for refreshments or revisit some of the bars in the evening. Otherwise, finish the walk here (you are only a 2-minute walk away from the start point, which you can reach by crossing to the far-right corner of the square and turning right along Charlotte Street).

Az walk four

A Waterside Walk

Along the Main Line canal to Edgbaston Reservoir.

Landlocked and possessing no sizeable river, Birmingham would not have become an industrial powerhouse without its famous waterways. And the rumours are true: Birmingham really does have more canals than Venice, at least in terms of mileage! What remains is one of the most intricate canal networks in the world, which can make traversing the inner city surprisingly calm.

This walk begins and ends around the buzzing canal basins of the city centre, where houseboat residents live amongst the Saturday night revellers. You will walk along the Main Line canal and end up at the tranquil setting of Edgbaston Reservoir, where you can catch a glimpse of the glimmering golden chaitya of the Peace Pagoda, a Buddhist temple.

As you arrive at the reservoir, take note of the Edgbaston Waterworks Tower and Perrott's Folly, both just off Waterworks Road. The angular Waterworks Tower, built in 1870, imposed quite an impression on a young J. R. R. Tolkien and thus inspired the citadel atop Minas Tirith in *The Lord of the Rings*. The second of the two towers, Perrott's Folly, is over 100 years older and has become part of Brummy folklore, with tales of its eccentric owner building the tower to look yearningly at his wife's grave.

start	Gas Street Basin, off Bridge Street
nearest postcode	B1 2JZ
finish	The International Convention Centre (ICC), Broad Street
distance	5¼ miles / 8.5 km
time	2 hours
terrain	Paved roads and paths. Some narrower paths, steps and short, steep slopes.

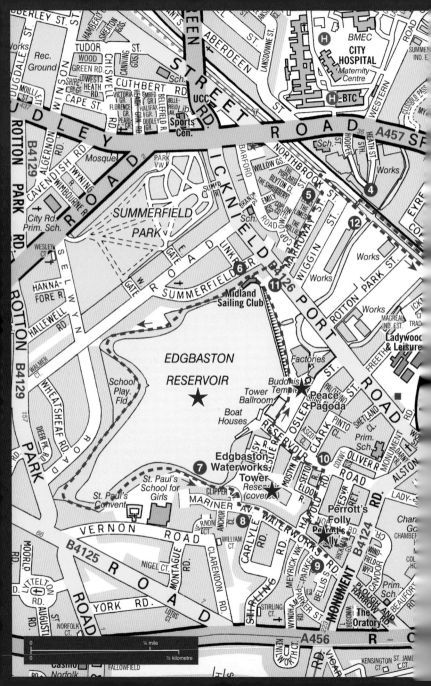

① As you turn off Bridge Street, follow the signage to 'Gas Street Basin' ★ down the cobbled ramp. Pass The Canal House on your left and continue to follow the path through the corridor of moored canal boats and over the small iron bridge. This narrow waterway underneath the steep bridge didn't used to exist. Instead, cargo was unloaded from boats on the Mainline Canal Line to your right and reloaded onto new boats already waiting on the Worcester & Birmingham Canal Line to your left. It wasn't until 1815 that an Act of Parliament opened the bar and a lock was built with the facilities to take a toll at the point of crossing. (If the path is blocked please see step 6 of walk 1 on page 11 for alternative directions.)

② Turn left as you come off the steep iron bridge (not the exit onto the street) and follow the canal path beyond the underpass – watch your head! Keep going along the canal path for about 5 minutes. You'll pass Brindleyplace ★ on your left (up the steps), a thriving destination in the evenings. A little further along – just as you come to the corner, known as the Old Turn Junction, as the canal sweeps round to your left – you'll see a pub called The Malt House across the way. Fun fact: during a break from the 1998 G8 Summit, US President Bill Clinton enjoyed a pint and a plate of chips with some bewildered Brummies at this fine institution.

③ Stay on the canal path, veering to the left until you come to a bridge that crosses you over to Arena Birmingham ★ on the other side. Take the ramp back down to the canal path and continue in the same direction as before. Walk under the next bridge, past Legoland Discovery on your right, and along the canal for a good 20 minutes (¾ mile / 1.2 km).

④ Take the fourth footpath bridge you encounter to cross the canal (just after where the two canals intersect). Once over it, turn right and continue along the canal until you discover some black railings to your left which lead to a sloped path to take you up to street level.

⑤ Emerge from the colourful metal railings and turn left onto Northbrook Street and continue until you can turn right onto Marroway Street. Follow this road right down to the end, where you will come to a main road (Icknield Port Road) with the play park on your left. Cross the main road and turn right to continue along it until you come to a sign on your left welcoming you to Edgbaston Reservoir. Enter here and continue past the Midland Sailing Clubhouse.

⑥ You have arrived at Edgbaston Reservoir ★. Built in 1827 by Thomas Telford and formerly known as Rotton Park Reservoir, it is still used for its original purpose: topping up the canals. You can fish here and also enjoy rowing or sailing as provided by the local clubs. Turn right as you approach the water and follow the path that circumnavigates the reservoir.

7 There will be opportunities to exit the path and reservoir as you walk but ensure you stay on the path until the third opportunity arises (past the rowing club on your right, just as you approach the car park ahead). Take this footpath exit up through the woodland and the small housing estate of Clipper View. Turn left out of here onto Mariner Avenue.

8 Continue down Mariner Avenue until it becomes Waterworks Road after the mini-roundabout. It is here that you can spy the Edgbaston Waterworks Tower ★ on your left. Continue past the tower and down the road until you encounter a car park (for Karis Medical Centre). You will be taking the footpath to the left of the entrance to this car park but before you do, sneak a peek at Perrott's Folly ★ just behind it.

9 Follow the footpath through the housing estate until you come out onto Hickman Gardens. Turn left then left again onto Noel Road, and make your way back towards the reservoir. When you come to the end of this road, turn right onto Harold Road and cross over when possible. Continue down Harold Road until the very end, where it meets Reservoir Road.

10 Turn left and carry on for 5 minutes until you are reunited with the reservoir. You should access the reservoir path through the Tower Ballroom car park; the Tower Ballroom was originally built in 1827 and functioned as an ice rink before being converted into a ballroom in the 1920s. As you meet the reservoir path once again, go right to continue your lap of the water. Keep walking until you meet the straight of the promenade (look out for the Peace Pagoda ★ on your right at the corner) and carry on to the end.

11 At the end of the straight, you will find yourself at the same entrance to the reservoir that you originally used. Exit this same way back onto the main road of Icknield Port Road. Cross over and then turn right down the road and retrace your steps back to the canal via Marroway Street on your left. Turn left onto Northbrook Street and find the steps through the colourful metal railings down to the canal path once again. Turn right onto the canal path and enjoy the same route you took to the reservoir from another perspective.

12 Without crossing over, continue on the canal path for around 25 minutes (1 mile / 1.6 km), back towards the city centre.

13 As you approach Brindleyplace, on your right this time, you can either take the steps up to enjoy the bars and restaurants or go over the bridge to your left to enter The ICC ★, home to the famous Symphony Hall.

Az walk five

Art in the City

The vibrant neighbourhood of Digbeth.

Digbeth has long been a part of Birmingham's industrious heritage; it was central to the early market trading days of the 12th century and later became a major manufacturing hub for the city. Today the area hosts a plethora of independent businesses, particularly within the creative and digital sector. With the neighbourhood embarking on an enormous fifteen-year development programme, now is the time to take stock of the grittiness that makes Digbeth so special.

This walk immerses you in Digbeth life. Edgy music venues nestle under the arches of the towering railway viaducts. Victorian corner pubs host football fans on match days whilst cocktail bars with table tennis attract a younger crowd. Restored factories contrast with modern sculptures to create vibrant spaces filled with al fresco hospitality. At Digbeth's centre remains the Custard Factory, which was built in 1906 by Alfie Bird for his family's famous egg-free custard business. Occupying 15 acres, it now hosts a gallery and cinema.

Unfolding at every turn is the famous street art which is governed by the rule: don't go over something if you can't paint something better! Veterans rub along with plucky newcomers to put their stamp on this unique part of the city centre. You will soon understand Digbeth's 2018 title as the 'Coolest Neighbourhood in Britain'. Hidden gems along this circular walk are provided by two Victorian public conveniences, a cunning fox and a railway to nowhere.

start / finish	St Martin's Church, Bullring
nearest postcode	B5 5BB
distance	2½ miles / 4.2 km
time	1 hour
terrain	Pavements and paved footpaths, some uneven.

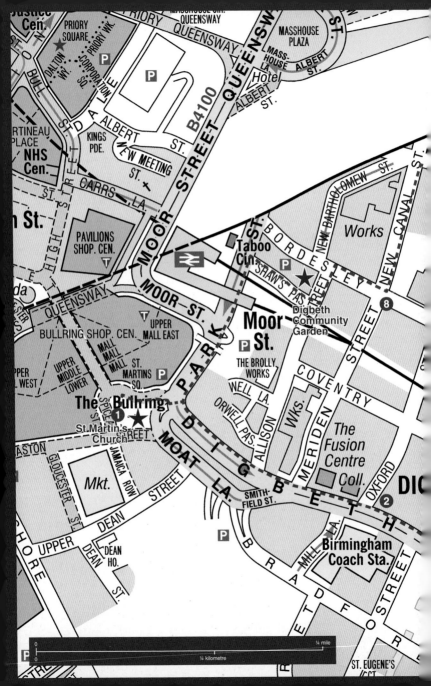

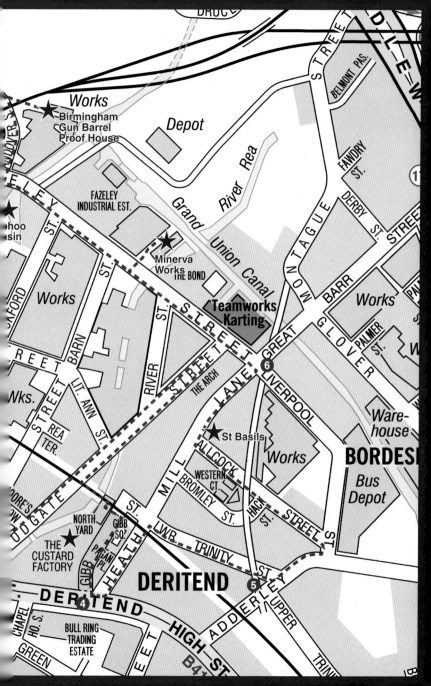

❶ This walk begins in front of J. A. Chatwin's most famous church – St Martin in the Bull Ring ★. Whilst most of this church was built in 1873, there has been a church on this site since 1290. Look for the outdoor 'Miller's Pulpit' under the spire – the only one of its kind in the country. With your back to the entrance, turn to your right to walk around the north side of the church and down the slope, with the iconic Selfridges aluminium discs on your left. Cross over the roads in front of you to join the left side of Digbeth High Street for about a third of a mile (0.5 km). Look out for the green tiled ghost sign atop 135–6 to George Makepeace's Clothing Mart, built in 1923.

❷ Continue past the Coach Station on your right and you will shortly see another ghost sign at number 85. The lintel above the entrance reads 'Bonser & Co' and, in true Digbeth fashion, is now a vintage clothes shop. You will then pass the Digbeth Institute which opened as a church in 1908 but is now a prominent music venue. Look at the six female sculptures by Gibbs and Canning: one is holding a purse representing the charitable funds that established the church and two are holding instruments in an entertaining example of foreshadowing. Have a brief peek into Milk Street on the left to see a restored ghost sign featuring Melox Marvels dog biscuits. Continue up the High Street and take the next left onto Floodgate Street. On the corner you can see the JFK Memorial. Created in 1968 by prominent Birmingham artist Kenneth Budd, it was moved to this location in 2013 to recognize the area's strong Irish Catholic history. It was restored by Kenneth's son, who maintained the wrong years for JFK's presidency.

❸ Be sure to walk slowly down Floodgate Street to take in the street art. Unmissable on the right is the Custard Factory's industrial chimney. On the left is a unique school designed by leading Victorian architects Martin & Chamberlain in 1891. The handsome building is built higher than the others in the city due to the small site. Walk under the railway arch and further down the street to check out great independents including Redbrick Market and The Ruin. Turn back down Floodgate Street and, beneath the railway arch, take the walkway to the left, over the River Rea. Follow it onto Gibb Street and the heart of the Custard Factory ★. Explore this whole site, being sure to take in the Courtyard and Tawney Gray's imposing Green Man sculpture.

❹ Keeping the Custard Factory on your right, exit Gibb Street onto the High Street, then turn left and take the immediate next left. On the corner is The Old Crown pub – the oldest secular building in the city, dating back to 1368. Thankfully it was saved three times from destruction by the Municipal Corporation. On the other side of the street is the Deritend Free Library; look out for the obligatory 'Forward' motto on the tallest gable. Walk under the viaduct arch and turn right up Lower Trinity Street. Lit up at night and awash with nightclubs and music venues, this is one of the most exciting streets in Digbeth. You can't miss the Marvel-ous street art in the car park on your left.

5 Continue to the end. The railway arch you pass under belongs to Duddeston Viaduct, a Victorian elevated railway line that never carried a single train. The project was abandoned, but there are now confirmed plans to convert it into a park in the sky. Turn left onto Adderley Street and left at the roundabout onto Liverpool Street. Then take the immediate left onto Allcock Street and walk its entirety. Opposite the end of the road is Eastside Projects, an artist-run free gallery with an eclectic exterior. Turn right onto Heath Mill Lane and pass the Romanesque St Basils ★ . Opened as a church in 1910, it is now a charity combating youth homelessness. At the junction with Fazeley Street, look at the far-right corner to see three listed cast iron Victorian urinals, the first of two on this walk.

6 Turn left down Fazeley Street. After 220 yards (200 m), on your right is Minera Works ★ , an art gallery that has a hidden gem. Accessible at most times of the day, enter through the black gates and continue straight to the canal. On your right is one of Annatomix's iconic geometric foxes. Turn back onto Fazeley Street and continue past three listed terraced

houses dating to 1840 and now looking fantastically out of place. Look to your left as you cross over the canal to see the Typhoo Basin ★ . This basin enabled the famous Birmingham tea brand to prosper, aided by marketing that emphasized its medicinal qualities: 'The tea that doctors recommend'.

7 Depending on progress with HS2, you may be able to take the next right onto Andover Street. Then turn right on Banbury Street and look through the gates to see the Jacobean-style gateway to Birmingham Gun Barrel Proof House ★ . This was established by law to guarantee the superior quality of the Birmingham Gun Trade. Retrace your steps, turn right onto Fazeley Street and left onto New Canal Street.

8 Take the first right onto Bordesley Street and the next left onto Allison Street. Under the railway arch on the left you will find another set of Victorian urinals, much better preserved than the others. Turn back and go left, up Shaw's Passage. On your right is another hidden gem, Digbeth Community Garden ★ , which regularly hosts events and welcomes all kinds of involvement. Turn left at the end, into Park Street, and walk under the railway bridge to return to St Martin's Church.

⚎ walk six

Second City Derby

St Andrew's to Villa Park.

At either end of this walk are the clubs of the 'Second City Derby', an intense football rivalry between Birmingham City and Aston Villa that has been going strong for over 140 years. Southeast of the city centre, Birmingham's modern St Andrew's stadium sits on top of Small Heath, which has been popularized to the world by the BBC drama *Peaky Blinders*. 'Bluenoses' revel proudly in the flat-cap culture and there are reminders of this era for those that look hard enough. Villa Park, undeniably a much grander stadium, sits in the grounds of the 1635 Jacobean stately home Aston Hall in the north of the city. This has been accessible to the public since 1858, when Queen Victoria performed the opening ceremony during her first ever visit to Birmingham. It's partly these contrasting settings that have fueled the stereotypes of class differences between the clubs.

In between these destinations is a walk that confronts Birmingham's devotion to the motor vehicle. Get past the ring road and you'll be rewarded with the oldest railway terminus in the world, soon to be rebirthed with HS2. You'll walk through Aston University's mid-century campus with brutalist gems still to be found. The Birmingham & Fazeley Canal saves a walk along the Aston Expressway with the eleven locks of the Aston Flight providing quiet passage through the urban sprawl.

Both stadiums are served by buses to and from the city centre.

start	St Andrew's Stadium, Cattell Road, Small Heath
nearest postcode	B9 4RL
finish	Villa Park, Witton Lane, Aston
distance	5 miles / 8 km
time	2 hours 30 minutes
terrain	Pavements, paved walkways and canal towpaths.

1 Begin your walk outside St Andrew's Stadium ★ on Cattell Road, looking at the mural by street artist Gent 48 of club legends Trevor Francis and Jude Bellingham, who was part of England's dynamic Euro 2021 team. You will also see the Kop Stand, which opened in 1994. Walk down Cattell Road past the club shop on your right and turn left onto Coventry Road. Continue past the retail park, then turn left onto Green Lane. Directly in front, you can see the stunning Green Lane Masjid ★ , incorporating the exterior of the former Small Heath Public Library (1894) and Baths (1902). The decorative circular clock tower dominates. Look at the adjacent library gable to spot the relief sculpture of medieval figures representing Learning, Knowledge and Study.

2 Bear left to walk down Little Green Lane, past the tiled frontage of the Cricketers Arms, and turn left down Arsenal Street. At the end, cross over the road and walk straight ahead down Camp Street to the end. Turn left onto Garrison Lane. You'll see the Blues pub, the Royal George, on the corner of Tilton Road complete with BCFC badge, Peaky Blinders mural and another image of Trevor Francis.

3 Walk past the Holme Estate on your left, a rare interwar attempt at flat building by the Council. Whilst then considered a failure, and nicknamed 'The Barracks' by locals, it is now of

architectural interest with Dutch-style design and mansard roofs. Continue along Garrison Lane for ¼ mile (400 metres) until you reach Witton Street. On the far corner is The Garrison ★ , the alleged former drinking hole of the Peaky Blinders gang. Now closed and in a sorry state, in 2013 actor Cillian Murphy came here to immerse himself in the Small Heath area and improve his accent in preparation for his role in the *Peaky Blinders* television drama.

4 Turn left onto Witton Street, follow it to the end and turn right on Lower Dartmouth Street. At the end of the street on your left you'll find a disused Victorian factory building with a handsome city coat of arms bearing the city's motto 'Forward'. Turn right and cross Garrison Lane then take the next exit off the roundabout onto Lawley Middleway. Cross at the pedestrian crossing and continue along Lawley Middleway until you reach the Curzon Circle roundabout.

5 Turn left onto Curzon Street. Walk straight down and take a moment to enjoy Eastside City Park ★ in front of Millennium Point. On your left is Curzon Street Railway Terminus – the oldest in the world – which opened in 1838 and which will be revitalized when HS2 arrives in the city. At The Woodman (1897), turn off the road and walk into the paved area. The pub was designed by prolific architect brothers James & Lister Lea; keep it on your left.

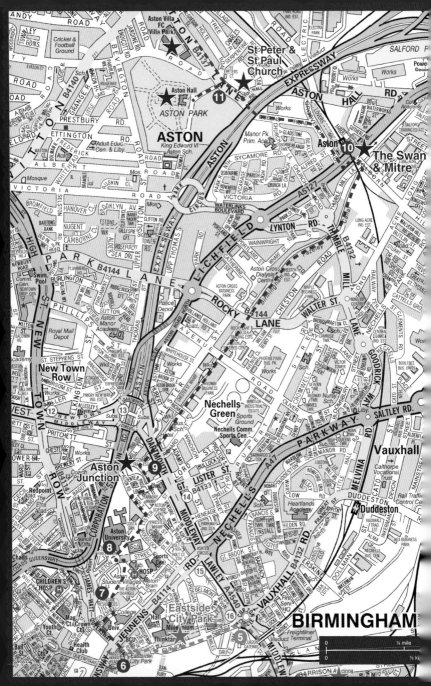

6 Turn right up Park Street. Walk up and over the pedestrian crossing onto James Watt Queensway before turning right onto Coleshill Street. Enter the campus of Aston University at the earliest opportunity. Walk around the left side of the lake. The pyramidal Peace Sculpture (1985) at the centre of the lake commemorates the workers killed in the air raid on Small Heath's BSA factory in 1941.

7 Take the path in between the rows of seats at the piazza. Keep the glass and brick library on your right – less architecturally striking since refurbishment but still attractive. Continue walking so that the imposing main building is on your left. As you pass, spot the last remaining concrete Aston Stones sculpture by John Maine on the grass on your left. Dating from the 1970s, local legend was that the five sculptures changed locations overnight.

8 Continue through the campus to the Sacks of Potatoes pub. Emerge onto Woodcock Street to the right of the pub. Bear left and take the first left at Holt Street, the first right at Love Lane, and then walk over the canal bridge before heading right, down the canal towpath and right under the bridge.

9 Continue along the towpath to Aston Junction ★ , which was once bustling as the main link between Birmingham's canals and the London Canal via Warwick. Turn right before the footbridge. Walk for approximately 30 minutes (1¼ miles / 2 km) along the Birmingham & Fazeley Canal, past 11 locks of the Aston Flight. At lock 11, just after passing under the railway bridge, turn off the towpath onto Holborn Hill and turn left. Another surviving James & Lister Lea pub, The Swan & Mitre ★ , is on the corner.

10 Turn left onto Lichfield Road and take in the seated statue of Britannia atop the pub of the same name. Cross over at the pedestrian crossing in front of it and proceed forwards onto Grosvenor Road, which leads onto Queens Road and then onto Witton Lane under the A38. On your right is the Church of St Peter & St Paul ★ , with its soaring 198-foot (60-metre) spire. Try and spot the gothic gargoyles on the pinnacle representing the Seven Deadly Sins.

11 On the opposite side of the road is the entrance to Aston Park. Walk through the gate and up the drive to view Aston Hall (1635) ★ , described romantically by Oliver Fairclough as 'a stranded relic of Birmingham's rural past'. Retrace your steps to Witton Lane and turn left. In front of you is the lavish matchday drinking hole The Holte (1897), brilliantly restored by the club's owner. Finish your walk behind this at the impressive and iconic Holte End of Villa Park ★ , rebuilt in 1994 to look like the now-demolished historic Trinity Road Stand.

ᴀᴢ walk seven

Towers, Tracks and Tennis

The affluent suburbs of Harborne and Edgbaston.

In the 19th century, Birmingham's industrial development was rapidly expanding outwards, but the powerful Gough-Calthorpe family refused to allow factories near Edgbaston Hall. This quirk of history resulted in the spacious and exclusive area explored on this walk.

Perhaps surprisingly, Edgbaston was handed over in 1957 to legendary Birmingham architect John Madin – of Central Library fame – to draw up a masterplan for the Calthorpe Estate. With so many of his brutalist buildings purged from the city centre, this walk offers a relatively intact tour around an ambitious mid-century vision of modern life.

The circular walk starts on Harborne High Street, 4 miles (6.6 km) southwest of the city centre, and takes in one of Birmingham's best urban trails. The Harborne Railway once saw thirty trains a day thunder along its tracks in the early 1900s. Now it is a beautifully scenic passage leading from Harborne into Summerfield. You will pass J. R. R. Tolkien's school The Oratory, through the business district and around Edgbaston's mix of grand architectural styles. Some of the city's most influential residents lived amid the suburb's Georgian townhouses and Greek-revival villas, from George Cadbury to the Chamberlain family. Where else in Birmingham would lawn tennis have been invented but this peaceful, historic neighbourhood?

start / finish	High Street, Harborne (near the junction with York Street)
nearest postcode	B17 9NJ
distance	8 miles / 12 km
time	3 hours
terrain	Pavements and gravel paths.

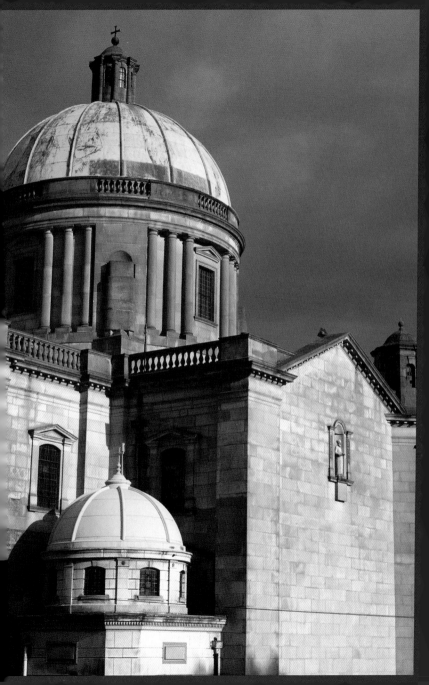

Harborne High Street can be reached by bus from the city centre. Parking is available at St John's Road car parks.

1 Start outside the grand Victorian former school, built by architects Martin & Chamberlain, which now functions as a lively food market called The School Yard ★. Cross over High Street at the pedestrian crossing, turn left and then right down Station Road. The baroque tower you can see is the old fire station. Walk past Clarence Road and take the next right onto Gordon Road. Take the left onto Rose Road and continue to the end. Turn left into Park Hill Road and go left again after the bridge, then take the next left into Forest Drive.

2 Take the signposted 'Harborne Walkway' path in the far-left corner of the cul-de-sac and continue for its entirety (1½ miles / 2.4 km). You will cross over an old railway bridge and then walk alongside the Harborne Nature Reserve ★ and Westfield Road Allotments. This route follows the Chad Valley, which gives its name to the famous Harborne toy company. You will pass under five bridges including the fun circular tunnel under Hagley Road.

3 Emerge into the open green space of Summerfield Park. Seek out the spectacularly grand Summerfield bandstand ★ near the far end of the park. This red-brick structure was built in 1907 and was most often used as an outdoor theatre. Come back on yourself and take the first exit to your left (East Gate) onto Gillott Road.

4 Turn right and walk past Christ Church (1885) ★, designed by prolific Birmingham architect J. A. Chatwin. Just before the junction with Selwyn Road, take the unmarked path on your left which takes you down to Edgbaston Reservoir ★. Turn right and walk in an anticlockwise direction along the west side of the reservoir. Take the first exit to the right, onto Rotton Park Road.

5 Turn left, cross over Portland Road and continue down Rotton Park Road. Take the first right onto Lyttelton Road and walk a loop around St Augustine's Church (1868) ★. Designed by J. A. Chatwin, this is the city's tallest church, its Gothic spire reaching 185 feet (56 metres). Retrace your steps as far as Portland Road and cross over, taking Vernon Road in front of you. On the left at the bend is Midland House ★, which was built around 1880 'to be a temporary asylum for women, fallen into habits of vice, who profess themselves penitent'. Continue round to Clarendon Road. Halfway down on your right are five grand houses, the most notable being the gothic villa at number 20 and number 18, with its coach house.

6 Turn left onto Hagley Road. Walk past the old St Chad's Hospital and the row of shops. Pass historic The Ivy Bush pub with its corner clock. After another 55 yards (50 metres), look for the impressive dome of The Oratory ★ looming into view. This catholic community was founded by John Newman in 1849.

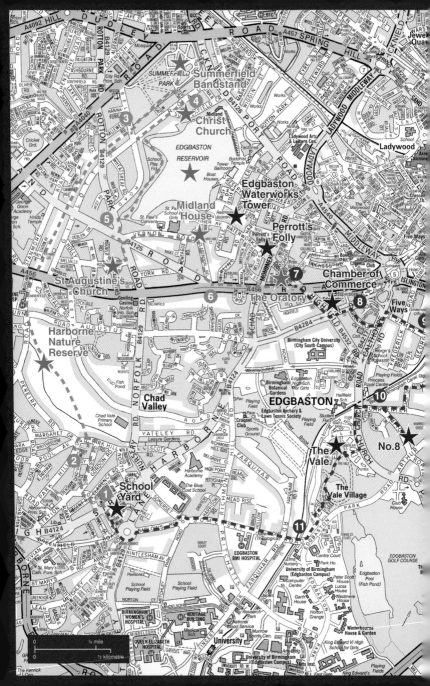

7 Cross over the Plough and Harrow Road (looking left for a view of Tolkien's Two Towers – Perrott's Folly ★ and Edgbaston Waterworks Tower ★), pass the historic gothic hotel and cross Hagley Road at the pedestrian crossing. Continue straight over, down Highfield Road. Keep an eye out for Tolkien's blue plaque on the front of Highfield Nursery. On the left at the corner of Harborne Road is the endangered Chamber of Commerce (1960) ★ , built by the brutalist architect John Madin. Immune to listing due to alterations, lovers of mid-century art should ask to see John Piper's mosaic in the main foyer – the staff may also point out his signature. Turn left onto Harborne Road.

8 Take the first right onto Greenfield Crescent directly opposite the crisp glass box design of Madin's Neville House (1976). This street underwent pedestrianization works in 2021 to make it the centrepiece of Edgbaston Village. There is an artisan market on selected Saturdays. Turn left on Calthorpe Road and take the first right onto St James' Road. Continue down the road and on the far-left corner at the intersection with Frederick Road is a much better preserved vision of office-working by Madin, one of fourteen postwar office buildings listed in England.

9 Continue down St James' Road, past George Cadbury's home at the corner of George Road, and turn right onto Wheeleys Road. Take the third

right onto Estria Road to see Madin's vision of a residential suburban street. Follow the road round to Cala Drive. Emerge onto Carpenter Road. The tower you can just about see on your far left is also a simple Madin conception. Turn right.

10 Tennis lovers should take a brief detour left on Ampton Road to see number 8 ★ , where lawn tennis was invented in the back garden (only the house is visible). Return to Carpenter Road and continue to the end, then turn left onto Church Road. Take the first road right just before student accommodation Chamberlain Tower. Enter The Vale student village ★ . Take the path along the right of the conservation area and cross the footbridge over Chad Brook. Walk in between the Mason accommodation blocks and then along the Mason Way footpath. Continue in the same direction until you emerge onto Somerset Road close to the junction with Edgbaston Park Road.

11 Turn right on Somerset Road. Continue straight on at the first roundabout and at the next roundabout take the second exit onto Barlows Road. Continue to the roundabout and take the third exit onto Greenfield Road. Turn right immediately onto York Street, which will lead you back to The School Yard.

ᴬᶻ walk eight

Survivors of the Postwar Clearance

The inner-city district of Nechells.

On this walk, you will discover some of the lost architectural gems that are being imaginatively repurposed. Nechells was once an incredibly densely populated area with terraced housing crowding around busy factories. After the Second World War, derelict housing was aggressively redeveloped. This walk takes in the stranded beautiful buildings from that 19th-century cosmopolitan community and explores the area's rich culture today. Nechells is home to Birmingham's poet laureate and teacher, Casey Bailey, who represents the area passionately. This walk will take you through the titular setting of Casey's first pamphlet, *Waiting at Bloomsbury Park*.

The standout hidden gem on this walk is the old Bloomsbury Public Library. Now teetering beside a dual carriageway, intricate sculptures by Benjamin Creswick portray everyday life for the communities that once lived here. One of the most important locations of the city's radical history, you will walk along the site of The Battle of Saltley Gate, where 15,000 workers forced the closure of the fuel depot gate during the 1972 miners' strike. From the historical to the bizarre, you will also see a pub that proudly appeared on TV's *Britain's Toughest Pubs*, featuring a punter who placed his false eye in his drink to prevent it from being stolen.

The walk begins at the railway station in Duddeston, an inner-city area to the northeast of the city centre. There is a regular train service from Birmingham New Street.

start	Duddeston Railway Station, Duddeston Mill Road
nearest postcode	B7 4ST
finish	Aston Railway Station, Lichfield Road
distance	2½ miles / 4 km
time	1 hour
terrain	Pavements and paved paths, moderate incline.

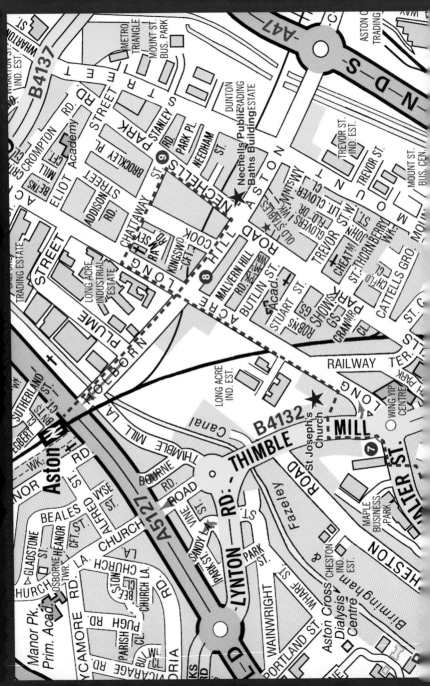

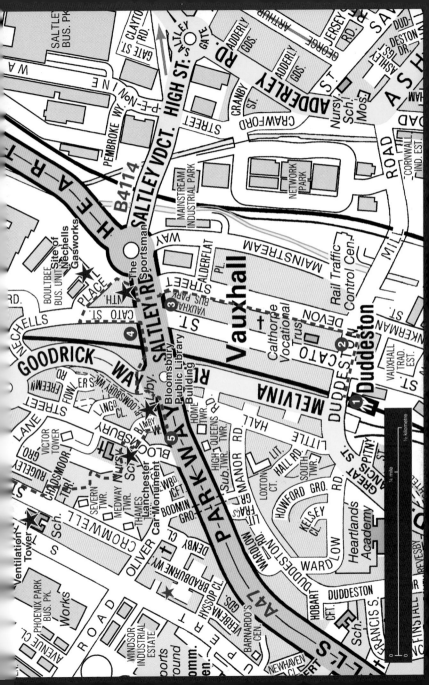

1 Exit Duddeston Railway Station onto Duddeston Mill Road and turn right. The road is named after the cornmill that was owned by the Holte family (of Aston fame) that sat along the River Rea. Take the second left onto Devon Street.

2 Walk all the way up Devon Street. Now lined exclusively with warehouses and industrial units, the east side once featured the 18th-century Duddeston House, home of Lunar Society member Samuel Galton. Ostensibly a Quaker, Galton was heavily criticized by members of his Meeting House for his involvement in gun manufacturing and the slave trade.

3 Turn left onto Saltley Road and cross over at the pedestrian crossing. Turn right. On your left is The Sportsman ★ pub, which was featured in the noughties television programme *Britain's Roughest Pubs*. Turn left off the roundabout into Nechells Place, which is blocked to traffic here. This was the location of Nechells Gasworks, scene of the 1972 Battle of Saltley Gate, where trade union president Arthur Scargill declared victory for the miners from above a block of toilets. Near the top of the road, you'll find the well-preserved corner pub the Albion Vaults, complete with gold Mitchells & Butlers logo – a firm favourite of local factory workers. Turn left down Cato Street North. The dramatic depiction of urban decay on your left was originally built to produce malt for local breweries.

4 Turn right, back onto Saltley Road, and walk under the viaduct. Cross over Goodrick Way at the pedestrian crossing and take Nechell's Parkway from the roundabout. Walk to the clocktower end of the pink terracotta building you can see. Originally Bloomsbury Public Library ★ , now a daycare centre, it was built in 1893 and is one of Birmingham's least-photographed architectural gems that deserves more recognition. The sculptured reliefs above the windows are by the prolific Arts and Crafts sculptor Benjamin Creswick. The large sculpture shows Art, Craft and Industry presenting their wears to Birmingham, represented by a female figure. However, the more striking tympanums are the smaller ones showing everyday working-class life including scenes of sports, labour and domesticity. Briefly look across the road at the three tower blocks. The one in the middle is Queens Tower, the first tower block built in Birmingham in 1954.

5 Now walk up Bloomsbury Walk next to the old library and emerge onto Bloomsbury Street. Cross the road and enter the park. On your left is the Lanchester Car monument ★ by Tim Tolkien, commemorating the genius of Frederick Lanchester and the cars that were produced locally in 1895. Take a right at the monument, then the next left and then continue along the path to exit onto Chadsmoor Terrace. Turn left. The attractive ventilation tower ★ in front of you belongs to Cromwell

Primary School. It was built in 1889 and designed by J. A. Cossins, who also designed Balsall Heath Public Baths. Turn right onto Cromwell Street and emerge onto Rocky Lane.

6 Cross over the road and take the footpath in between Camrose Tower and St Joseph's Primary School. Walk briefly down Brough Close to the left and take the first pedestrian walkway to the right, along the front of the houses. Take the left as the path forks away from the houses and walk down to Walter Street and cross over the road. In front of you to the right is the Wing Yip superstore, the original store of the Chinese supermarket chain founded by Woon Wing Yip. Walk towards the roundabout.

7 Take the path round to the left, down Thimble Mill Lane. To your left is the towering local landmark of Aston Manor Brewery. Cross over the road and proceed up the path to St Joseph's Church ★. Built by Pugin in 1850 and enlarged by his son in 1872, look out for the interesting, stylized statues of Mary and Joseph flanking the entrance. Walk through the grounds to the right of the church and emerge onto Long Acre under the lychgate. Turn left and proceed for a quarter of a mile (400 metres) until arriving onto Holborn Hill. Turn right.

8 Walk down Holborn Hill to the crossroads with Nechells Park Road. To your left is The Villa Tavern (1925). On the far-left corner is the grand Nechells Public Baths (1910) ★, now home to The Wisdom Cultural and Islamic Centre, its entrance flanked by two turrets with open cupolas. Carved lettering shows the male and female entrances, and the coat of arms is again by Creswick. Turn left and walk down Nechells Park Road. On your right are some of the only residential properties that survived the postwar clearances.

9 Turn left onto Chattaway Street. In the distance ahead you can see Aston Parish Church and Villa Park. Turn left onto Long Acre. Take the next right onto Holborn Hill and continue down until you arrive at Aston Railway Station.

A–Z walk nine

In the Footsteps of the Lunar Society

The northwestern suburbs of Handsworth and Soho.

The tale of the Lunar Society, an 18th-century dinner club, represents the foundation story of the City of Birmingham. The group is named because the learned industrialists and intellectuals would meet on the night of the full moon so they could navigate home successfully. This walk retraces the inebriated steps of these towering figures around the suburbs of Handsworth and Soho, on a short circular walk.

Commencing at the 'Cathedral of the Industrial Revolution', 3½ miles (5.6 km) from the city centre, you will see impressive murals of the titans of industry that lived and worked around Soho. You will then see the manifestation of civic pride while walking through the Victorian Handsworth Park, past a boat house once set alight in the Suffragettes' struggle for women's voting rights. Hidden gems are found in the relief panel on Handsworth Library that tells a tale of industrial espionage, and the lost gatehouse of James Watt's home. This walk is packed with great architecture and thriving high streets in an area that is a monument to the industrial age.

There is a regular bus service between the city centre and Hamstead Road.

start / finish	St Mary's Church, Hamstead Road, Handsworth
nearest postcode	B20 2RW
distance	3½ miles / 5.6 km
time	1 hour 30 minutes
terrain	Pavements and paved paths.

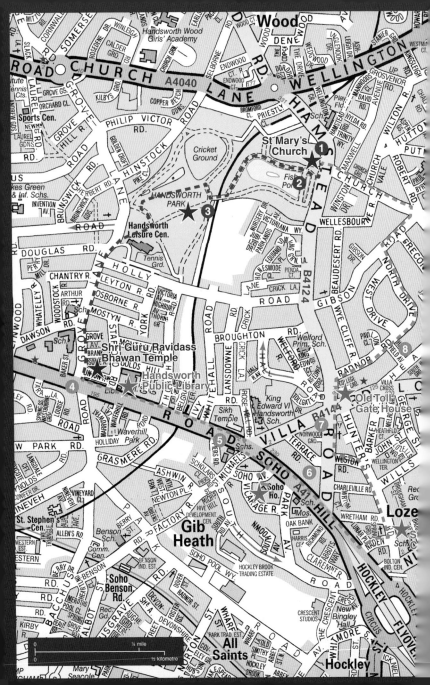

1 Start at St Mary's Church ★, which is the resting place of some of the most famous figures from the industrial age. Enter and you will see three striking murals of James Watt, the inventor who made the greatest improvement to the steam engine, William Murdoch who invented gas lighting, and Matthew Boulton, the practical industrialist and head of the Lunar Society who realized their ideas. You will see that one of the children underneath the bust of Boulton is holding an engraving of the Soho Manufactory which pioneered mass production. Football fans can pay homage to George Ramsay – 'Founder of Aston Villa' – who is buried in the churchyard. Exit the church and turn right onto Hamstead Road. Take the next pedestrian right into Handsworth Park ★, one of the finest parks in the city, which was born out of the municipal activism that was a feature of Birmingham in the late 1800s. A novel aspect to this park is that it is cut in two by the railway, with each half having a distinctive character.

2 Continue straight along the path so that the pond is on your left. One local legend is that of the 'Handsworth Pike'. Anglers used to fish the pond in the early 1900s but were dismayed to be catching fewer and fewer fish. A great pike was rumoured to be eating them and a reward of a month's wages was offered to anyone who could catch it. After months of failed attempts, a local man called Morton caught the pike

and proudly displayed its taxidermied form in a glass cabinet in his home. Turn left at the far end of the pond with Luke Perry's *SS Journey* – representing the hopes of those making the sea crossing from Jamaica destined for Handsworth in the 1960s – on your right. Walk to the right of the boathouse, rebuilt after the original was set on fire in 1913 by Suffragettes. Take the bridge over the railway.

3 Take the next right and turn left past the restored Victorian bandstand. Continue all the way down the path and turn left at the Sunken Garden. The large building in front of you is the leisure centre. Make your way down towards it and walk around it, keeping the building on your left. Emerge onto Grove Lane and turn left. Walk down the well-preserved Victorian high street with fruit and vegetables displayed attractively outside the stores. Vanley Burke – considered the godfather of Black British photography – had his first studio on this street. Continue past the squat-looking Church of St Peter, one of J. A. Chatwin's last in the city. You will pass Handsworth Grammar School, with its attractive bell tower turret, which counts broadcaster Adil Ray among its alumni. Continue past the brilliantly ornate Shri Guru Ravidass Bhawan temple ★ on your left.

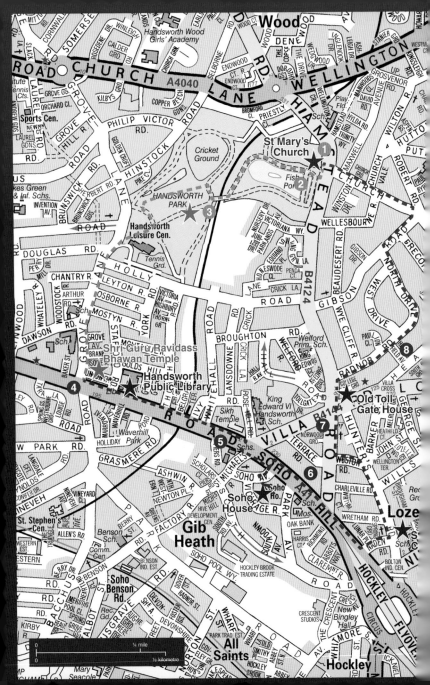

4 Turn left onto Soho Road. On your left after 55 yards (50 metres) is the triumphant Handsworth Public Library building (1879) ★ . The relief panel on the first turret on your left depicts a tale of industrial espionage in stone. Carved by legendary local sculptor Benjamin Creswick, Watt and Boulton are in conversation about an advance in the steam engine whilst a man in the background, Dick Cartwright, is eavesdropping and would give their secret away. Continue on Soho Road.

5 After a third of a mile (500 metres) you will pass the striking Sikh temple on your left. Cross Soho Road at the pedestrian crossing then cross St Michael's Road and stay on the main road (now Soho Hill) as far as Soho Avenue. Turn right and take the next left to arrive at Matthew Boulton's classical home, Soho House ★ . This was the regular venue for the Lunar Society to discuss the future of industry and society, and is now a museum. Retrace your steps to Soho Hill and cross back over the road.

6 Continue down Soho Hill, crossing Hamstead Road at the crossing and taking the next left onto Naden Road. Follow Naden Road to the end and you will emerge onto Hunter's Road. The intricate Tudor-Gothic St Mary's Convent ★ is in front of you, built in 1841 by Pugin of St Chad's Cathedral and the Palace of Westminster fame. Turn left and walk up to the quaint corner pub, The Observatory. Turn left onto Weston Road and at the end, turn right onto Hamstead Road.

7 Continue past Villa Road and the Arts and Crafts Asian Resource Centre, formerly the Old Toll Gate House ★ , occupying the site where tolls were collected from stagecoaches as traffic increased in the early 18th century. Check out the doorway on the Villa Road side for intricate panelling and glasswork. Continuing up Hamstead Road, take the next right onto Radnor Road. Halfway along on your left you will see a blue plaque on the former gatehouse to James Watt's home, Heathfield Hall. So Boulton and Watt were business partners, friends and even neighbours!

8 Continue around to the end of the road. Turn right into Gibson Road and then, at the junction, turn left onto Church Hill Road where St Mary's Church will return into view.

A **Z** walk ten

A Century of Architecture

The University of Birmingham's Edgbaston campus.

The University of Birmingham was the first of the nine 'Red Brick' universities to be granted independent status and its stunning Chancellor's Court did much to popularize the term.

A practically minded institution keen to do things differently, the University tasked Aston Webb and Ingress Bell to design the original buildings, and they purposely chose a different architectural style to the colleges of Oxbridge. The campus is now a trove of Victorian, Sixties brutalist and modern buildings with sculptures hiding behind every corner.

Concrete lovers will revel in Muirhead Tower and Ashley Building whilst fine art lovers need to drop into the Barber Institute. The hidden gem? Roary the T. rex. This walk navigates up to the tranquil Vale and then uses the Worcester & Birmingham Canal to return to the start.

start / finish	University Railway Station, Westgate, Edgbaston
nearest postcode	B15 2FB
distance	3 miles / 4.8 km
time	1 hour 15 minutes
terrain	Pavements and paved walkways, canal towpath and steps.

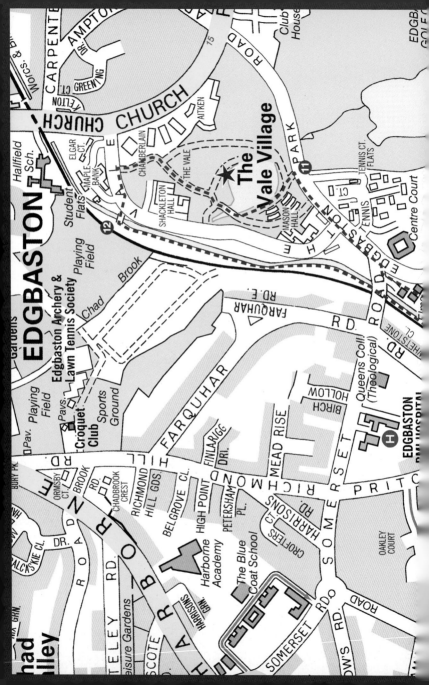

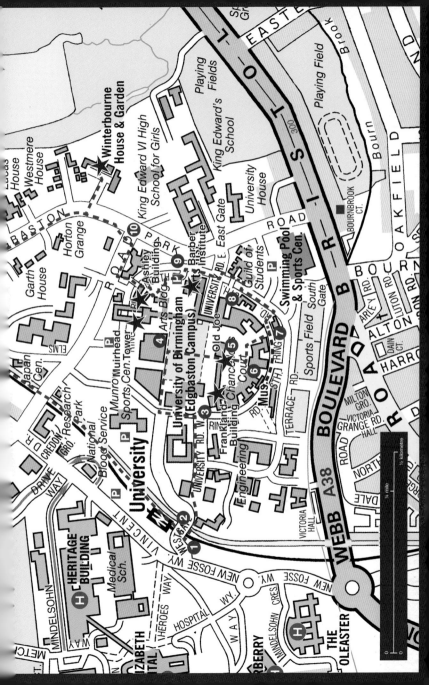

1 Start at University Railway Station, recently redeveloped to handle the increase in footfall during the Commonwealth Games. If completed, you can take the steel pedestrian bridge over the canal. Otherwise exit onto Westgate and turn left over the bridge. On the left you will see a sign providing information on the Roman fort that once stood here on the old Roman Road. It was constructed soon after the Roman invasion of Britain in AD 43 and had towers, timber walls and double ditches to aid with defence.

2 Across the road from the Roman site, walk past the Faraday statue sculpted in 2000 to celebrate the University's centenary. Michael Faraday, who discovered the laws of electromagnetic rotation, is seen here with loops of bronze between his hands. Walk down the steps in between the buildings on the attractively landscaped path. Continue along the side of University Road West. The red brick building in front on your right is the 1908 Frankland Building ★ and the first sight of the Webb and Bell semicircular masterplan.

3 Turn left so the University Centre is on your right. Turn right between the shop and gleaming £60 million library with gold detail. This will open up into the heart of campus. In front on the left is brutalist masterpiece Muirhead Tower (1969) ★ . It has more detractors than admirers and topped University news website *The Tab*'s

ranking of the ugliest buildings on campus in 2020. Regardless, Downson's building competes with the Signal Box for the best remaining brutalist building in the city.

4 Walk to the middle of the path and then turn right down the steps, noting the University crests behind the wall. In front is the Joseph Chamberlain Memorial Clocktower, or 'Old Joe' ★ for short. Standing at 325 feet (99 metres), it's the tallest free-standing clock tower in the world and was inspired by Siena's Torre del Mangia after Chamberlain saw it whilst on holiday in Italy. Continue down through University Square and underneath the clock tower. Beware: there is a superstition that any student walking under the arches when it chimes will fail their degree!

5 You will emerge at the centre of Chancellor's Court (1900–1909), the University's main hub and an impressive Byzantine conception. In front is the Great Hall which was intended to act as a 'Cathedral to Learning'. As well as being the ceremonial hub of the University, it has twice helped the country face healthcare crises. Firstly, as a hospital during the First World War and more recently as a Covid-19 test centre.

6 Continue to the Great Hall. The statues are to titans of Arts and Science and most should be familiar. Chancellor's Court was unfinished for over a century – with two domes on the right and only one on the left – until the Bramall Music Building completed the symmetry in 2012. Look out for the ceramic friezes atop the original buildings representing the subjects first taught inside. Turn left and take the pedestrian way to the right, in between the two domes. Look behind you for another great view.

7 If you want to see a Tyrannosaurus rex called Roary, turn right and follow the semicircular road round until you arrive at the free Lapworth Museum of Geology. Afterwards, retrace your steps to rejoin the route. If you are not visiting the museum, simply turn left and take the next path to the right, down the sloped path. Turn left and walk up the road.

8 Take the steps on your right up to the Student Guild. Inside the quad is Mermaid Fountain by Birmingham sculptor William Bloye (1960). Exit the quad by the same way and turn immediately right. Cross over the road, and again, so that you are by the sign saying 'Ring Road North'. Continue along this road. The refined Barber Institute (1939) ★ is on your left. Free to enter, the interior flows around the central auditorium and contains works by renowned artists Gauguin and Van Gogh.

9 Take the next road left and walk across the car parks to the circular Ashley Building (1964) ★, uncompromisingly Sixties with its precast exterior panels. Be sure to

look inside if you can! It is much softer with a glorious circular staircase. Brutalist fans should spend a bit of time exploring this part of the campus. Walk so that the Ashley Building is on your left, up the steps and over the pedestrian bridge. Continue along the path and turn right on Pritchatts Road, walking to the end.

10 Turn left onto Edgbaston Park Road. After 55 yards (50 metres), on your right is Winterbourne House (1904) ★, an Edwardian villa with fantastically varied gardens. Continue up Edgbaston Park Road for half a mile (800 metres). When you see the lake on your left, enter The Vale student village ★.

11 This beautiful set of University 'halls' amid gracefully contoured parkland was initiated in the Fifties after the University realized it had the highest number of students in private houses than any provincial university in the country. The result is a surprisingly bucolic setting for a city university. Proceed in a clockwise direction around the lake, over the bridge and turn off towards Chamberlain Tower. Walk beneath it, keeping it on your right and turn left onto Mason Way. Walk down and take the next right turn in the road, through the car park and over the canal bridge.

12 Turn left onto the towpath and enjoy one of the greenest stretches of canal in the city. Follow the Worcester & Birmingham Canal for one mile (1.6 km), all the way back to University Station.

⒜⒵ walk eleven

Bohemian Birmingham

Moseley and Balsall Heath.

The word 'bohemian' may be an overused cliché when it comes to describing Moseley, but it's certainly one that is hard to dispense with. Packed full of historic pubs and hosting jazz and folk festivals, this suburb's name has become a working adjective. Bumping into a rock star at the farmers' market? So Moseley. Having a pint in Tolkien's old haunt and stumbling on a crowded ukulele gig? So Moseley. An impromptu dance on 'Bog Island' after a Michelin-starred meal? So Moseley. The area's distinctive character is actively conserved and enhanced by the Moseley Society, formed over 40 years ago.

Commencing on the high street of this suburb, located 4 miles (6.4 km) southeast of the city centre, you can revel in the pub history and ghost signs of businesses gone by. It's then down Ladypool Road, the centre of the Balti Triangle. In Balsall Heath you will pass the stunning Library and Baths before returning up Moseley Road to finish. Plan this walk for the last Saturday of the month to experience the lively farmers' market and open access to Moseley Park.

start / finish	The Fighting Cocks, St Mary's Row, Moseley
nearest postcode	B13 8HW
distance	2½ miles / 4 km
time	1 hour
terrain	Pavements, moderate incline.

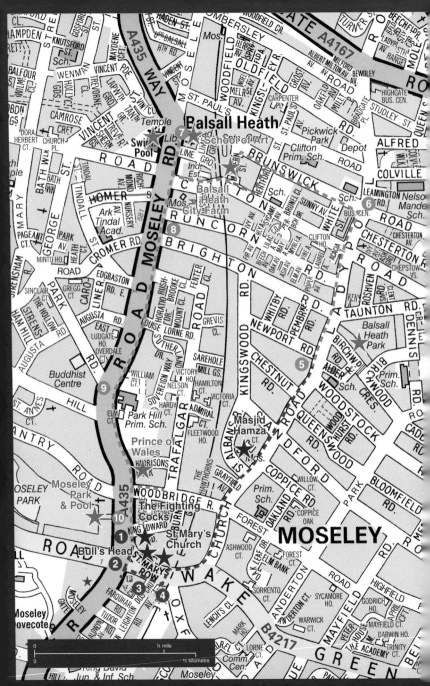

Buses from the city centre set down on Alcester Road close to the start point. Alternatively, car parking is available in Moseley Village Car Park off Alcester Road.

① Start outside The Fighting Cocks ★. A pub of this name has been here since at least 1759 when, on Boxing Day, a cock-fighting contest took place with a winning prize of £10. The current building was completed in 1899, boasting an octagonal tower with in-built barometer and anemometer at street level. Cross over to the triangular village green, more commonly referred to as 'Bog Island' after the old underground public toilets. Trams would circle around the village green before returning to the town centre. Cross over St Mary's Row at the pedestrian crossing and walk to the corner, currently occupied by the cocktail bar Bohemian. This site was where the horses employed on the busy tram route were stabled. The current building was built in 1906 and hosted the Tramways company offices.

② Walk past Bohemian and along to 174–176 Alcester Road, which is currently a newsagent. Above two windows are decorative bricks with key detail carved in. This is the logo of the Municipal Bank and the building used to be the Moseley branch. Return to St Mary's Row and walk along it without crossing the road.

③ Over to your left, the Bull's Head ★ is the oldest pub site in Moseley and dates back to 1700. Pass The Elizabeth of York, named after the wife of King Henry VII, who donated the land opposite for St Mary's Church. This pub was opened in 2006 despite strong opposition from the local 'No More Pubs' campaign. A year later the area was declared a 'Saturation Area' which blocked more licensed premises from being established. Pass the charming Church Avenue with rows of terraces either side of a path. Just above the entrance you can see part of a ghost sign to Lilian Freeman's 'home handicrafts, needleworks and fancy leathers' business.

④ Use the pedestrian crossing to cross back over St Mary's Row. In front is St Mary's Church ★. The site dates to the 15th century but has been much altered, most significantly by the prolific Chatwins (father and son) in the late 19th and early 20th century. The church bells were replaced in 2012 after being branded the 'worst sounding in Britain'. Continue up St Mary's Row and turn left at Church Road. Starting at number 118 is an incredibly attractive row of terraces circa 1840. Cross over Woodbridge Road. The building on the far-left corner is the old school and school master's house (1851). Continue on, towards the metal dome of the Masjid Hamza ★. Previously at 15 Woodstock Road, it was one of the first mosques in Birmingham.

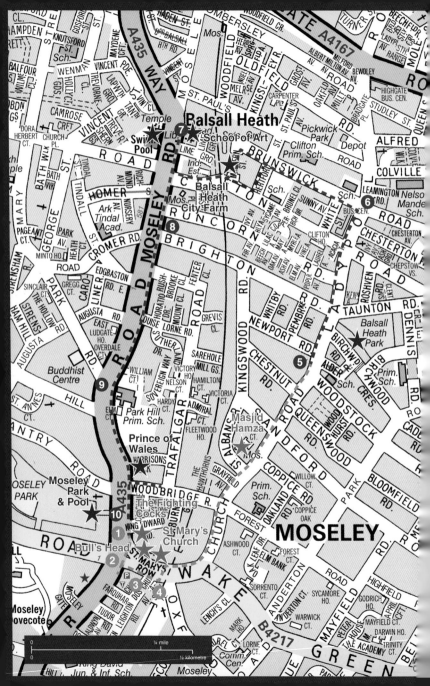

5 After the mosque, the road narrows and becomes bustling Ladypool Road, which is at the heart of the city's famous 'Balti Triangle'. At the corner of Taunton Road is Balsall Heath Park ★. The row of houses on the far side of the park is Birchwood Crescent, where nearly all the properties lost their roofs during the 2005 Birmingham tornado. Continue down Ladypool Road.

6 Turn left at Brunswick Road and walk to the end. You should be able to walk through the gate and across the path next to Balsall Heath City Farm ★ onto Clifton Road. The most urban farm in the city, it has been operating since 1980. If it is closed, turn around and take the first right down Hertford Street instead. Turn right onto Clifton Road. Continue to the end and turn right onto Moseley Road.

7 Walk down until level with the exquisite Balsall Heath Library and Baths ★. The north side is the library (1895) and has a striking terracotta clock tower. The baths is on the south side (1907) and, flanked by octagonal towers, is one of only five public baths in the country that are Grade II listed. Thanks to the passionate Friends of Moseley Road Baths community group, you can still enjoy a swim there. Opposite is the School of Art (1899) ★ with Arts and Crafts detail and doric columns. Famous alumni include musicians Christine McVie, Roy Wood and Ali Campbell. Next on the right is the Old Print Works. Turn back along Moseley Road.

8 Number 548 on the row of shops used to be Oriental Star Agencies. This record label played a crucial role in the development of Bhangra music in Britain when they signed the Bhujhangy Group, the world's longest-standing Bhangra group which was founded in Smethwick. Pass the crumbling listed tram depot and office building. As the road becomes Alcester Road, you will pass The Diwan Balti Restaurant where former Prime Minister David Cameron dined in 2012. You can still order 'The Prime Minister Special' off the menu.

9 Near the crest of the hill you will see the Tipu Sultan which was once The Jug of Ale music venue, hosting bands such as Oasis, The Verve and Moseley's own Ocean Colour Scene. Returning to the centre of Moseley you will pass the Prince of Wales ★, where the author J. R. R. Tolkien used to secretly drink with his girlfriend, out of sight of her mother. A brief detour down the next left, Woodbridge Road, will show you the 1870 Patrick Kavanagh pub just after a remaining 'Bakers' ghost sign, where Luker's long-standing Moseley Steam Bakery once was.

10 On the last Saturday of each month, you have the option to take a detour around Moseley Park & Pool ★, which is accessed via an alleyway between the shops on the right (look out for the arched sign above). Otherwise, continue along Alcester Road back to the start.

AZ walk twelve

The Three Parks

Connecting the parks of South Birmingham.

One of Birmingham's most surprising secrets is its prevalence of green spaces! In fact, the city is one of Britain's greenest cities. With ninety-three urban parks, a huge 15.6 per cent of the city is green. This walking route will connect you to three of South Birmingham's best parks: Kings Heath Park, Highbury Park and Cannon Hill Park.

Public parks emerged in Birmingham in the 1830s in a bid to improve the health of the working classes living in overcrowded conditions. In a rapidly growing industrial town, it was hoped that parks would reduce disease, crime, and social unrest, as well as providing 'green lungs' for the city. As a result of this organic evolution, each of the three parks on this walk has a very different feel. Kings Heath Park is closely connected to horticulture, Highbury Park is largely untouched and relaxed, and Cannon Hill Park is Birmingham's premier Victorian park with impressive floral arrangements and statues.

Beginning at Kings Heath Park 5 miles (8 km) south of the city centre, this walk is also dotted with curiosities including The Church of Scientology headquarters, a 16th-century pub rebuilt brick-by-brick, and a scale model of the Elan Valley in Wales.

start / finish	Kings Heath Park Car Park, Avenue Road, King's Heath
nearest postcode	B14 7TG
distance	7 miles / 11.2 km
time	2 hours 45 minutes
terrain	Pavements and some gravelled paths.

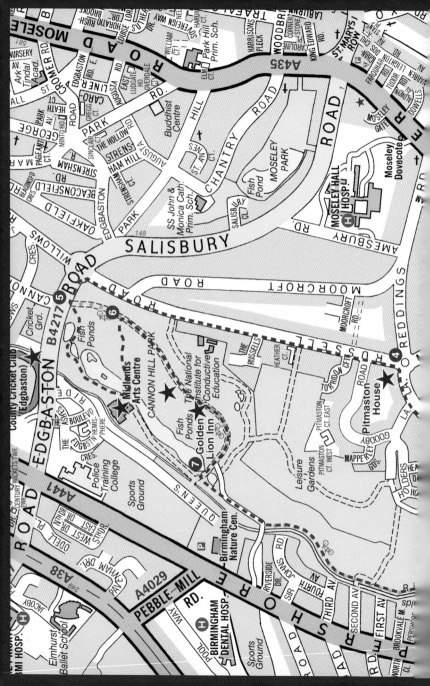

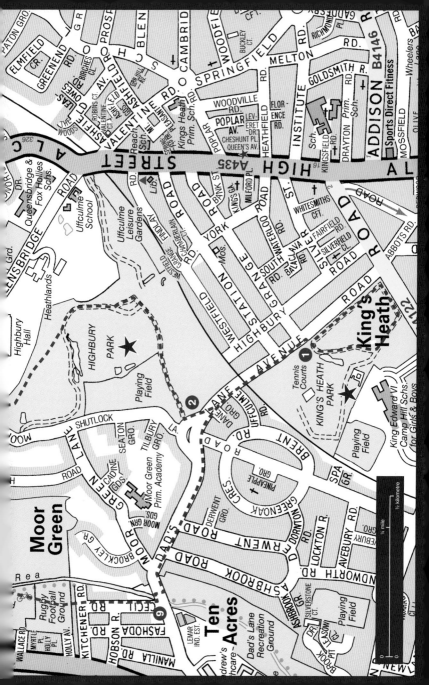

1 From the car park, enjoy a circular amble around Kings Heath Park ★. The central house was built in 1832 but the land around the house was not converted into a public park until 1908. The Television Gardens used to host *Gardener's World* and are open to the public twice a month. Exit onto Avenue Road and turn left. Continue straight down under the rail bridge, cross over when you get the chance and keep right onto Dad's Lane. Continue round the corner onto Shutlock Lane where you'll see the yellow entrance to Highbury Park.

2 Enter Highbury Park ★ and follow the paved road past the car park. When you meet a fork in the path, take the left and then turn left again onto the footpath. This large open park features both glades and woodlands. Be sure to visit the volunteer-led community orchard in the north of the park, with adjacent trails leading to Highbury Hall. Highbury Park used to be the grounds of Highbury Hall, a Grade II listed building and the estate of Joseph Chamberlain, former Lord Mayor of Birmingham. He left the park to the people of the city on his death in 1914; most of the grounds became a public park in 1930. With the eventual aim of exiting the park at the northwest corner onto Yew Tree Road, feel free to explore. If you can hear noisy bird song, it's almost definitely coming from the flock of parakeets that have made the park their home.

3 Once you exit the park onto Yew Tree Road, turn immediately right onto Moor Green Lane. Continue to the roundabout. On your left you will see the headquarters of the Church of Scientology in the Grade II listed neoclassical Pitmaston House ★. Take the first exit onto Russell Road.

4 Continue down Russell Road for about three-quarters of a mile (1.2 km) until you meet the mini-roundabout at the end of the road. Turn left and walk along Edgbaston Road. You'll see Edgbaston Cricket Ground ★ loom in and out of view; home to Warwickshire County Cricket Club, for years it had a novel motorized pitch covering nicknamed the 'brumbrella'. There is a black-gated entrance to Cannon Hill Park ★ on your left. Enter onto the footpath.

5 Birmingham's flagship park is named after the area which was the resting point of Royalist troops on their way to the Battle of Naseby in June 1645, during the English Civil War. The park first opened to visitors in 1873 after the land was donated to the people of Birmingham by major benefactor Louisa Ryland (whose blue plaque you should spot to your right upon entering the park). Firstly, take the smaller footpath to your right and keep right. You will reach the Japanese Gardens, complete with a 1961 scale replica of the Elan Valley in Powys, mid-Wales, from where the city famously draws its drinking water.

Now walk anticlockwise around the Canoe Pool. You are walking towards 'the MAC' (Midlands Arts Centre) ★ and should reach the end of the pool with it in front of you. Continue walking around the pool to your left until you can take the path slightly uphill. On your left is the Boer War Memorial. Keep going round to the park's main, wider path.

6 Turn right onto the main path and keep to the left as it forks. Continue past the original Grade II listed bandstand on your left which is the meeting point for Saturday's Park Run. You'll also walk past the Golden Lion Inn ★ on your right which is a 16th-century timbered house (originally from Deritend, Birmingham) that was moved and re-erected in the park in 1911. Even further along, to your left, you will find a smaller footpath leading to the Tunisian terror attacks memorial. The 'infinite wave' design has 31 threads, each representing a British national that died. Continue on the main walkway and round to the right.

7 Walk down over the footbridge over the large boating lake and take the first footpath left. Continue walking so that you pass a large sandy area of terrain on your left. Keep walking past this and take the footpath to continue straight for half a mile (800 metres), following the River Rea to your right. Count the footbridges over the river as you pass them.

8 When you reach the third footbridge over the river to your right, cross over and then continue along the path, keeping the river to your left now. Although small, this is the river on which Birmingham was founded by the Beorma tribe in the 7th century. You'll come out onto Pebble Mill Playing Fields, named so due to their proximity to the site where the well-known Pebble Mill BBC studios once stood. Continue on the path in the same direction until you can exit the park onto Kitchener Road. Cross straight over Kitchener Road and onto Cecil Road. Continue past all the glorious Victorian terraces of Cecil Road.

9 At the end of Cecil Road, turn left onto Moor Green Lane. Cross at the pedestrian crossing and continue along Moor Green Lane until you can veer right onto Dad's Lane. Follow Dad's Lane around the corner and all the way along until it turns into Avenue Road, just after the overhead bridge. Walk along Avenue Road until you reach the entrance to Kings Heath Park, which is where you began your walk.

A-Z walk thirteen

The Alternative Commonwealth Games Circular

Perry Barr and Witton.

'There's never been a better time for Birmingham to tell its story', according to *Peaky Blinders* creator and opening ceremony producer, Steven Knight, on the event that will change the city's image for generations of people. The focal point of the 2022 Commonwealth Games is the renovated Alexander Stadium, which features on this walk along with the athletes' village that never was, as well as a cemetery and an iconic landmark rarely traversed on foot.

This walk of contrasts starts in the northern suburb of Perry Barr, 4 miles (6.7 km) from the city centre. You will discover a charming lock-keeper's cottage hidden away from view. You will walk through Birmingham's largest cemetery with a spectacular chapel offering one of the best vantage points over the city, and where dignified war graves remind us of the shared history that the Commonwealth nations have beyond sport.

Approaching along the Tame Valley Canal, you will pass under north Birmingham's temple to brutalism: Spaghetti Junction. With the tangle of roads spiralling above, there is a surprising calm along the tree-lined canal-side. These are some of Birmingham's least-visited gems that offer a rewarding experience for the more adventurous explorer.

start / finish	Perry Barr Railway Station, Birchfield Road, Perry Bar
nearest postcode	B20 3JE
distance	7½ miles / 12 km
time	3 hours
terrain	Pavements, canal towpaths and uneven park paths.

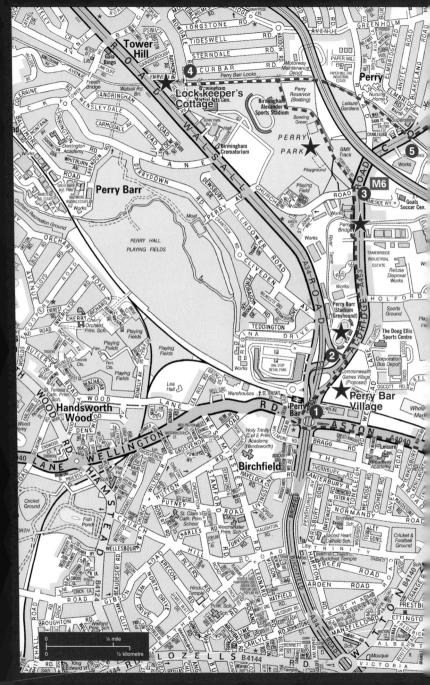

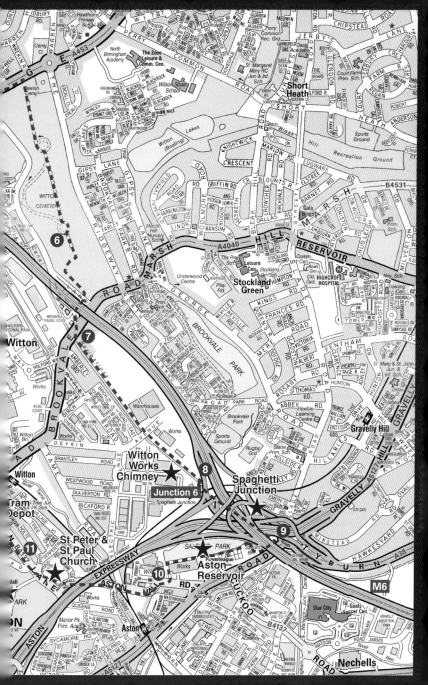

There is a regular train service between Birmingham New Street and Perry Barr. Alternatively, Perry Barr can be reached from the city centre by bus, which sets down on the main A34 road close to the railway station. If you are arriving by car, you may find on-street parking in the area to the southwest of the station.

1 Start at Perry Barr Railway Station. Turn left towards the retail park and cross the A34 at the first pedestrian crossing. Walk towards the new Perry Barr Village ★ on Aldridge Road. If open, look into this large residential scheme with open spaces and garden streets. This was originally intended to be the athletes' village before the Covid-19 pandemic delayed its completion.

2 Find your way back to Aldridge Road and cross over at the pedestrian crossing to see the Greyhound Racing Club ★ . During the Second World War, this stadium accommodated Italian prisoners of war and used to host athletics club the Birchfield Harriers. You can still see their logo, a running stag, on its facade. Rendered in art deco style bas relief, the stag was carved in 1929 by local sculptor William Bloye. Walk for about half a mile (800 metres), keeping on the pedestrian path as it diverges slightly from the road after Dairy Drive. You will walk over the Grade II listed Perry Bridge ★ which was commissioned in 1709. Constructed in red sandstone in a packhorse style, there has been a crossing on this spot since Roman times.

3 Follow the path back to the road and walk a little further until you enter Perry Park ★ on your left. Home to Alexander Stadium, the Commonwealth Games have caused a major re-landscaping of the park. Walk towards the stadium, labelled the best in the country by athletics legend Brendan Foster, then make your way to the Tame Valley Canal at the north end of the park.

4 It's definitely worth turning left and crossing over the Perry Barr Locks Bridge to reach the lock-keeper's cottage ★ built in 1834. It feels very quaint and almost rural. Turn back and cross back over the bridge. With the canal on your left walk along the towpath for about a mile (1.6 km), past the ten Perry Barr locks. At lock 10, walk up the slope on your right to join College Road.

5 Cross the road and turn left. Walk up College Road, across Moor Lane and continue up with Witton Cemetery on your right. Enter the cemetery through the metal pedestrian gate. You are now in one of the country's biggest cemeteries, covering 103 acres (0.4 square kilometres). Opened in 1863 and 'full to capacity' in 2013, it can be atmospherically beautiful on a clear day. For the most direct route, continue on the path in front until it takes you to the tree-lined main wide boulevard. However, it is interesting to wander, and the war memorial graves are worth seeking out.

6 The tree-lined main boulevard ends at the chapel, which is the highest point. You now have one of the best and most unique views of the city centre. Take the descending footpath on the far right-hand side of the chapel and navigate to the pedestrian gate. The contrast between the graves and the motorway on your descent is bizarre to take in. Exit the pedestrian gate and walk straight ahead, under the M6. Turn left and take the first right onto Brookvale Road. Cross over using the island and continue walking up the road. Before the bridge, turn down the path to your left to rejoin the Tame Valley Canal.

7 You will now walk along the canal for approximately one mile (1.6 km). The urban setting may look increasingly imposing but the path is well-used. The first thing of note after a short walk is another lock-keeper's cottage on the left. Shortly after, you will see the tall handsome industrial chimney ★ of General Electric Company's Witton Works factory which opened in 1902. The old magnet logos are still visible.

8 With the Gravelly Hill Interchange – the official name of Spaghetti Junction ★ – now looming into view, cross over the roving bridge to the right side of the canal and continue. The brick railway bridge contrasts nicely with the junction. Continue walking under the roads looking up at the tangle of concrete. You will walk through a long tunnel that, whilst lit up, is relatively dark.

9 Passing almost entirely under the junction, take the first towpath on your right before going under the Salford Bridge. Walk up the ramp and emerge onto Lichfield Road. Continue along Lichfield Road before taking the dirt footpath on your right towards Aston Reservoir ★ . Walk along the footpath and emerge beside the reservoir – another area rarely visited. Walk around with the reservoir on your right until you get to the far end. Turn left up the path and emerge onto Aston Hall Road.

10 Turn right to the roundabout then take the first exit and follow Aston Hall Road under the two railway bridges and the Expressway, and onto Witton Lane. For information on Aston Hall ★ , the Church of St Peter & St Paul ★ and Villa Park football ground ★ , turn to page 43.

11 Walk up Witton Lane past Villa Park on your left. Just before the roundabout on your right you can see the first purpose-built tram depot ★ in Birmingham, which was built in 1882. Cross over the roundabout onto Aston Lane and walk along the road for about three-quarters of a mile (1.2 km), until you rejoin the A34. Use the pedestrian crossing to the left of the roundabout to cross over, then turn right to return to the station.

ᴀᴢ walk fourteen

The Shire:
Tolkien's Childhood Playground

Moseley Bog and the Cole Valley.

This walk explores the leafy delights of a neighbourhood that once enchanted J. R. R. Tolkien and served as inspiration for his novels, *The Lord of the Rings* and *The Hobbit*. Tolkien drew on many aspects of his life in Birmingham to create the magical detail in his books, and here you will tread the same paths he did as a child. Described by Tolkien as a 'lost paradise', this area of Birmingham has become less rural than in the late 1800s but has maintained its bucolic charm.

This circular walk starts 5 miles (8 km) southeast of the city centre and takes you past Sarehole Mill, a 250-year-old Grade II listed water mill which is now a museum. It is thought to feature in *The Hobbit* when Bilbo Baggins ran 'as fast as his furry feet could carry him down the lane, past the great mill'. Plan your walk between Wednesday and Sunday and you can enjoy the freshly baked pizza served there! Nature lovers will enjoy the walk along the River Cole Valley – teeming with so much wildlife that even Eurasian otters have been spotted here. An equally rare curiosity, you will see seventeen fantastically preserved prefabricated bungalows on Wake Green Road. Originally built to last just ten years, they are still going strong and were Grade II listed in 1998.

start / finish	Moseley Bog Car Park, Windermere Road, Moseley
nearest postcode	B13 9JP
distance	3 miles / 5 km
time	1 hour 15 minutes
terrain	Pavements and trail footpaths. Parkland paths which can be muddy.

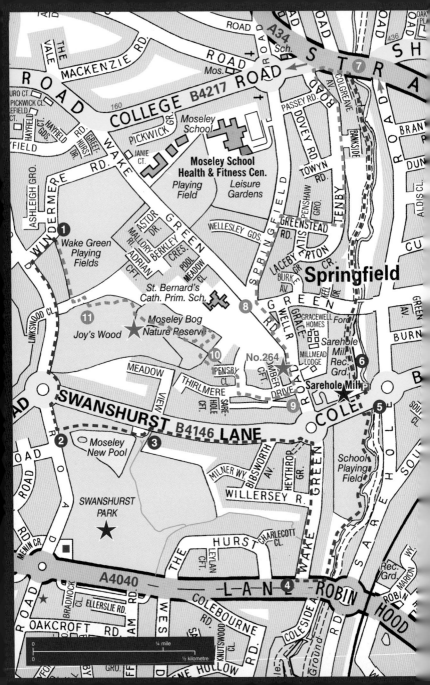

The walk starts at Moseley Bog car park and can also be reached by bus from the city centre, setting down on Yardley Wood Road a short way into the walk.

1 From the car park, turn left and walk down Windermere Road to the end, then turn left again onto Yardley Wood Road. Continue down Yardley Wood Road and then go straight over the roundabout to continue.

2 Immediately after the bus stop, you'll see a footpath entering a park on the left. Take this path to enjoy walking through Swanshurst Park ★, keeping on the path to the left of the lake. In 2017, so many Canada Geese settled in the park that there were calls to cull them after they terrorized the park users! Once you have walked the path along the edge of the lake, take the left footpath to exit the park out onto Swanshurst Lane.

3 Turn right onto Swanshurst Lane and continue until you reach the roundabout. Take a right turn past the Hungry Hobbit café and walk down Wake Green Road. Towards the end of the road on your left are the corrugated solutions to the postwar housing shortage. Built in the 1940s, Historic England said these quaint cream bungalows survive 'as a testament to postwar recovery, innovation and optimism for a brighter future.'

4 Turn left onto Brook Lane and take the first pedestrian turning left onto the John Morris Jones Walkway, named after a local headteacher and author. Surprisingly well covered, you'll hear creatures scurrying into the bushes along this ribbon of nature. Follow the trail alongside the River Cole.

5 Exit the trail and cross over Cole Bank Road. You can now see the tower of Sarehole Mill ★ looming above the trees. Still a working mill, Sarehole Mill has also been restored to a museum and welcomes visitors. Tolkien and his younger brother often explored the grounds here, nicknaming the miller's son the 'White Ogre' as he used to chase them away! Rejoin the John Morris Jones Walkway just past the museum, accessing it through the Sarehole Mill car park. As you leave the car park, opt for the left-hand footpath to take the small bridge over a stream.

6 Continue on the footpath and enjoy the scenery of the Cole Valley, which is part of The Shire County Park. In 2005, this area was renamed after 'The Shire' in *The Lord of the Rings* and *The Hobbit* to emphasise its importance and influence over the young Tolkien. As you reach Green Road, on your right is one of the few remaining fords in the city. Crossing the ford is not to be underestimated – in 2019 a 4x4 driver luckily escaped with his life when his car was swept and trapped under the bridge. Navigate through the gates, over the road and continue along the trail.

The Shire: Tolkien's Childhood Playground   89

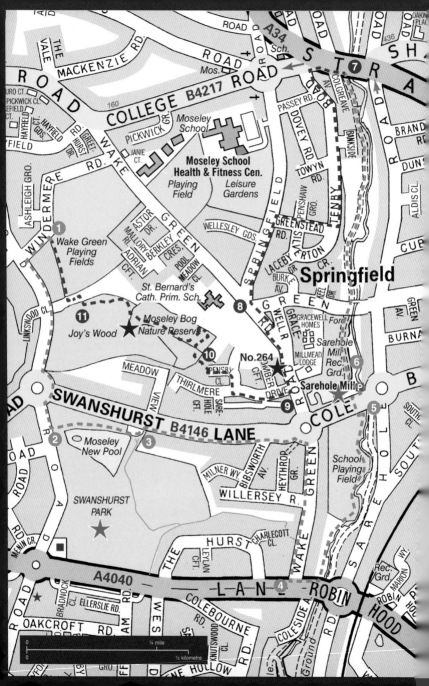

7 Continue all the way along the John Morris Jones Walkway and walk over the apple mosaic to exit onto Stratford Road. Turn left along the road and you will see the impressive Mughal-e-Azam restaurant in the converted Sparkhill United Church built in a Romanesque style during the interwar period. Continue past the restaurant, take the first left onto College Road and then turn left onto Tenby Road. Continue along Tenby Road and take the third right onto Greenstead Road. At the end, turn left onto Springfield Road.

8 At the end of Springfield Road, turn left onto the main road of Wake Green Road (ignoring the immediate left turn onto Green Road). Continue down Wake Green Road and cross over to the opposite side when you get the chance. Just after the bus stop, on the right, there is number 264 Wake Green Road ★. Formerly known as 5 Gracewell Cottages, this is where the Tolkien family lived from 1896 to 1990; the author remarked that these years were some of his happiest childhood memories.

9 Take the next right onto Thirlmere Drive. Continue until you can take the second right onto Pensby Close. As you get into Pensby Close, take the left fork. You'll see an access footpath past some cute bungalows into Moseley Bog – take this path.

10 As you approach Moseley Bog, take the right-hand path over a little bridge and follow the path into Moseley Bog ★ itself. Then navigate onto the elevated wooden path that provides safe passage over the perpetually damp woodland. Enjoy your surroundings – they were direct inspiration for Tolkien's ancient forests in his novels. Part of this area is Joy's Wood, named after local conservationist and campaigner Joy Fifer who saved the site from development in the 1980s.

11 Keep walking straight until you reach the part where Moseley Bog and the playing fields meet. Go up the muddy hill next to the old tree. Be careful, it can get slippy in the wet. Join the path into the playing fields and then keep to the left perimeter to follow the path back to the car park where you started. If you find that you come out at the Yardley Wood Road car park or one of the other exits, simply turn right and follow the road back up to find Windermere Road and the car park.

A/Z walk fifteen

Industrial Heritage and Civil Rights

A tour of Smethwick.

Saved from being incorporated into the city of Birmingham by a single vote, it was pride in Smethwick's contribution to history that kept it as a separate town. Yet at only 4 miles (6.2 km) west of the city centre, Smethwick's proximity to the city, both geographically and in terms of shared history, means that it can often feel part of Birmingham.

This circular walk joins the Main Line Canal as it carves through towering embankments towards the Black Country. The view over the awesome site of the Chance Brothers Glassworks provides just one example of productive capacity in a town famous for bicycles, pen nibs, rolling stock and screws.

The town's social history has been as remarkable as its industrial achievements. Postwar immigrants from the British Commonwealth were met with a hardened cruelty unusual even for the times. Smethwick was witness to what was possibly the country's most racist election when, in 1964, Peter Griffiths was elected Conservative MP with highly offensive unofficial campaign slogans. This prompted a visit from the civil rights activist Malcolm X, who walked purposefully down a street that had been set to become 'White only'. Nearby is The Ivy Bush. Once a segregated bar, today it is a thriving desi pub representing the soul of the town.

start / finish	Holy Trinity Church, Church Hill Street, Smethwick
nearest postcode	B67 7AH
distance	6 miles / 9.7 km
time	2 hours 30 minutes
terrain	Mostly pavements with uneven and sometimes muddy towpaths. Some steps.

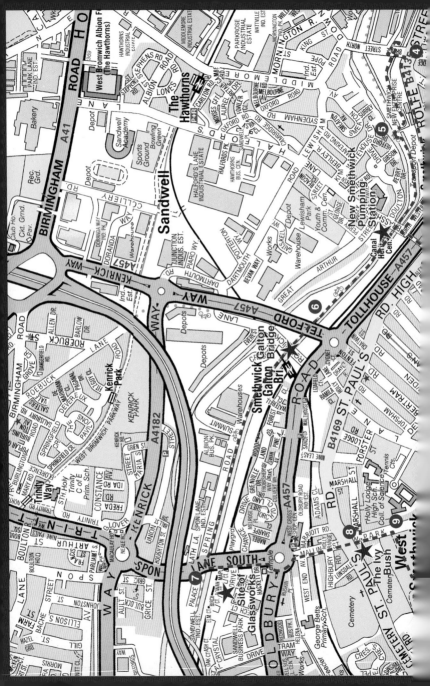

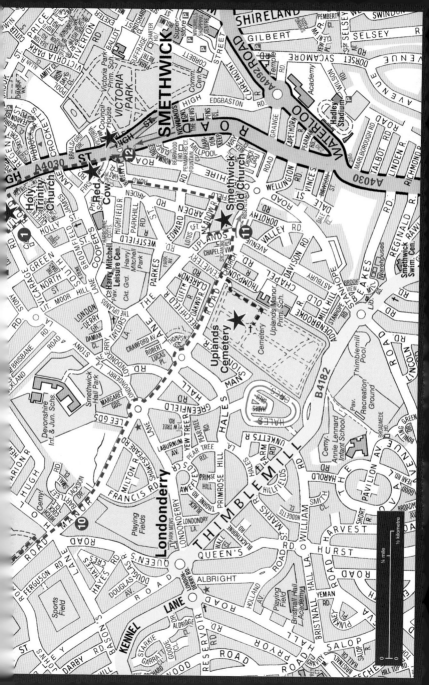

The start point may be reached by bus from the city centre, which sets down on High Street, or by train from Birmingham New Street to nearby Smethwick Rolfe Street. If arriving by car, there is on-street parking available on South Road alongside the church.

1 Begin the walk at Holy Trinity Church ★ on Church Hill Street. From the church gate with your back to the church, turn right and right again onto Trinity Street, and then left onto Smethwick High Street. You will see the Sikh temple Guru Nanak Gurdwara ★ which, having first been established in 1958, was the first Gurdwara in Europe and remains one of the largest.

2 Continue down High Street past Smethwick Library, which occupies the former Town Hall built in 1866. Next to this is the Blue Gates Hotel ★. Malcolm X, the US civil rights activist, stopped here for a drink during his visit on 12 February 1965. At the time, people of colour weren't allowed in the Lounge or Smoke Room. Attempting to order from the Smoke Room, Malcolm and his guide, Avtar Singh Jouhl, the General Secretary of the Indian Workers' Association, were asked to exit and order around the bar.

3 After Stony Lane, cross High Street at the zebra crossing. The 1820 tollhouse on your right has long been a fixture of what was the Birmingham, Wolverhampton and Dudley Turnpike. Use the pedestrian bridge to cross the A457 and railway line and after

descending the steps on the other side, proceed forwards along North Western Road. At the end, facing the train station, turn left onto Rolfe Street and continue for half a mile (800 metres).

4 At Bridge Street North turn left. The road takes you over the Engine Arm canal. Look for the gap at the end of the brick wall on the right-hand side of the road and take the steps down onto the towpath – beware, the path is muddy after rain. Turn right to go under the bridge you just crossed and continue along the canal side. The canal was built to feed James Watt's Smethwick Engine, the world's oldest working steam engine. From 1779, it pumped water up to the summit of the Old Main Line Canal. It is now at The Thinktank museum in Birmingham. Walk along the canal and cross the Engine Arm Aqueduct.

5 Cross over the bridge on your left but be sure to look right for a view of the Smethwick locks. Take the path sloping down to the left to join the canal you just crossed over. Turn right along the New Main Line Canal, but look behind you to see the cast iron aqueduct built by Thomas Telford in 1825. After about a third of a mile (500 metres) you will pass the New Smethwick Pumping Station ★, with its handsome chimney, which replaced the Smethwick Engine in 1892. It is now a museum open on select Saturdays.

6 Continue along the canal and through the Galton Tunnel. As soon as you emerge you will have the awe-inspiring sight of the Galton Bridge ★, built by Telford in 1829, and at the time the longest single-span bridge in the world. Continue along the canal for another third of a mile (500 metres) and take the first path right, up the embankment.

7 Turn left onto Spon Lane South. Looking over the side of the bridge on your right (you may have to stand on tiptoe), you can see what remains of the world's greatest industrial glassworks: Chance Brothers ★. These works made the lighthouse lenses that lit the world's sea lanes, as well as the opal glass of Big Ben and the panes of Crystal Palace. Still impressive despite being derelict, the site is being ambitiously regenerated. At the roundabout, continue onto Mallin Street. On the corner of St Paul's Road you will see The Ivy Bush pub ★. Once barring people of colour, it is now a friendly desi pub.

8 Cross St Paul's Road onto West Park Road and take the first left onto Marshall Street. Had racists prevailed in the 1960s, this street would have become all White, with the Council intending to let available houses only to White families. A blue plaque on the first house on the right commemorates Malcolm X's visit of solidarity, just nine days before he was assassinated in New York. Retrace your steps and continue down West Park Road.

9 At the first pedestrian entrance, turn right into West Smethwick

Park ★. Walking straight ahead you will soon see the James Chance Memorial on your right, thanking him for gifting the park to Smethwick in 1895. Walk through the park to the opposite side and exit onto Victoria Road. Turn left and follow it onto Manor Road.

10 On your right you can catch glimpses of the Sandwell Aquatics Centre, built for the 2022 Commonwealth Games. Continue straight down Manor Road for just over half a mile (1 km). If you still have energy, you may wish to take a walk around Uplands Cemetery ★. Continue along Manor Road as it changes into Church Road.

11 You will soon see Smethwick Old Church (1732) ★ on your left. This quaint church witnessed a small hamlet being transformed into an industrial boom town. Turn left to walk up The Uplands and pass The Old Chapel Inn. Turn right down Meadow Road and left on Rosefield Road. At the end of Rosefield Road, turn right onto Watery Lane. Cross over before the roundabout and walk onto Smethwick High Street.

12 Directly opposite the junction is the baroque-style Council House (1907) ★ to the left of the Victoria Park War Memorial. Turn left and follow the High Street for a third of a mile (500 metres), passing the local landmark the Red Cow ★. Finally, turn left down South Road to return to the starting point.

ᴀz walk sixteen

A Factory in a Garden

The model village of Bournville.

Named in reference to fashionable French chocolatiers, Bournville is the charming suburb created by George Cadbury from 1894 onwards. A Quaker and benevolent capitalist, Cadbury summarized his vision at the Rest House's 1914 unveiling as enabling all to 'enjoy the benefits of sunshine, fresh air and the beauties of nature'. This is evident on this circular walk around the elegantly designed model village that lies 5 miles (8 km) southwest of the city centre.

Central to this walk are the cottage-like houses designed by Cadbury architect William Harvey, who began in post aged just 20 years old. It's worth walking slowly along Sycamore Road observing all the variations of the semi-detached home, with decorative gables, first-floor front doors and dormer bungalows providing the most interest. You'll walk through the factory grounds where you're guaranteed the unmistakable aroma of chocolate as you approach the Bourn Brook. For secret delights, look out for George Cadbury's hidden statue, the original logo of Birmingham's Lloyds Bank and the railway bridge damaged in the Second World War.

Your companion throughout the walk will be the sound of the Carillon – a rare instrument in which bells are played by a keyboard – that sits atop Harvey's Bournville Junior School. Time your visit at 12:00 or 15:00 on a Saturday to hear a full recital!

start / finish	The Rest House, Bournville Village Green
nearest postcode	B30 2AD
distance	3½ miles / 5.5 km (+ optional ½ mile / 1 km)
time	1 hour 40 minutes (+ optional 20 minutes)
terrain	Pavements and paved paths. Gentle inclines, some steps.

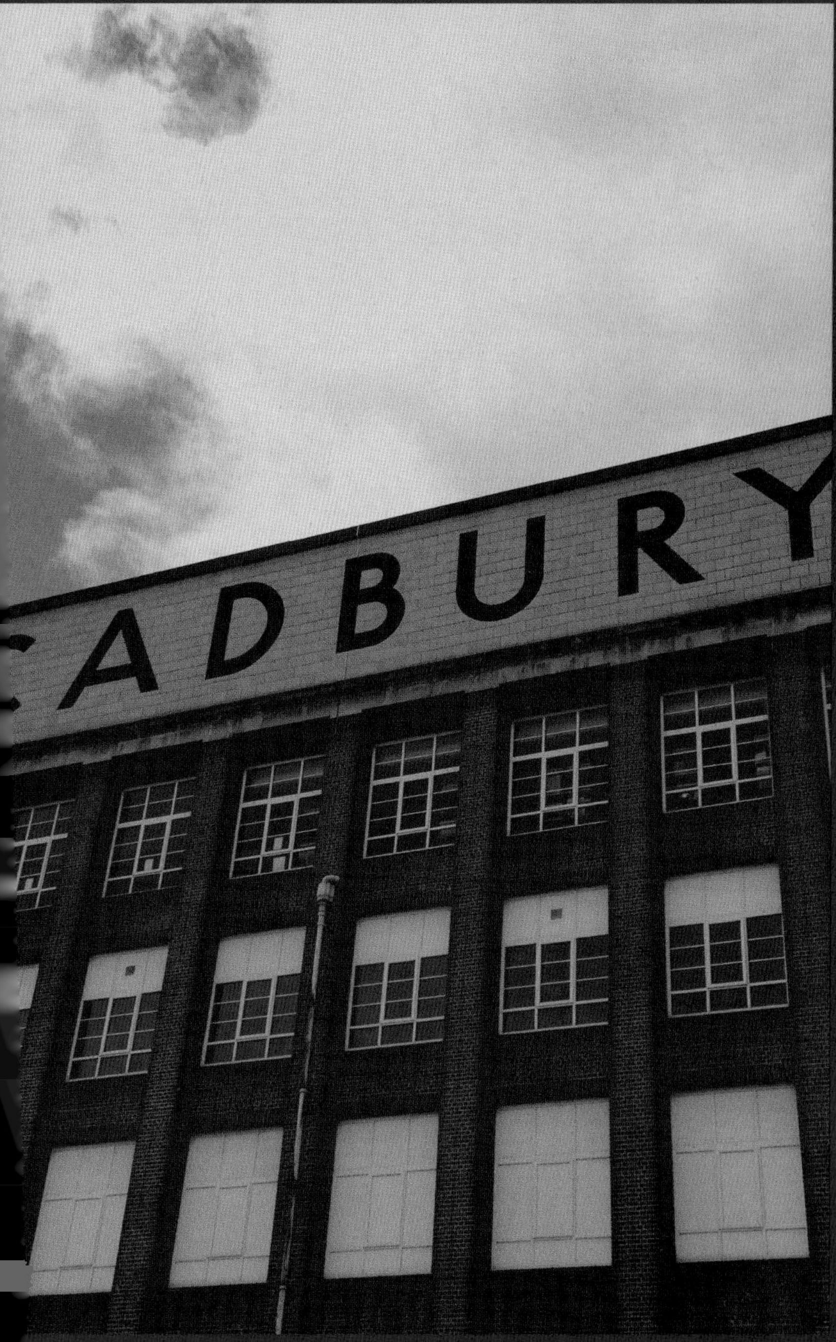
ADBURY

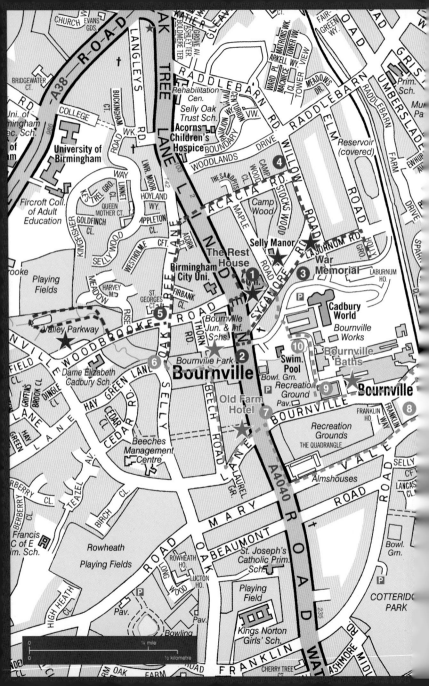

The starting point may be reached by bus from the city centre, which sets down close by on Linden Road. Alternatively, on-street parking is available on Sycamore Road. If you wish to arrive by train, there is a regular service between Birmingham New Street and Bournville Station – you would then start the walk at step 8.

❶ Begin your walk at the octagonal Rest House ★ in the middle of the green that was paid for by Cadbury workers to mark George and Elizabeth's silver wedding anniversary. Walk up the footpath to the Quaker Meeting House, ensuring you walk behind the hedge to the right of the building to see a hidden bust of George Cadbury. Go left down Linden Road. Cross at the pedestrian crossing and walk past Bournville Village Primary School, taking in the intricately carved leaves and vines on the arched entrances.

❷ Cross back over Linden Road and turn up Sycamore Road (you may prefer to use the pedestrian crossing just beyond the junction). Be sure to spot the beehive engraved above the old Lloyds Bank. This was their original logo before the black stallion. The black timber-framed Selly Manor ★ is on your left. Originally located on Raddlebarn Road to the north and dating back to Tudor times, it had fallen into disrepair until George Cadbury had it restored and reconstructed on its current site between 1912 and 1916. His son Lawrence said the building

would help the citizens of a new city like Birmingham remember 'bygone times'.

❸ Continue up Sycamore Road then make a short detour down Laburnum Road to the right, passing the war memorial ★ . Turn right into Holly Grove, one of the quaintest roads in the city, with houses designed by Harvey; one even has heart-shaped shutters. Retrace your steps and turn right along Willow Road before the war memorial. Continue straight ahead at the junction with Sycamore Road, to stay on Willow Road.

❹ Turn left up Acacia Road past charming bungalows and walk its entire length. Cross Linden Road and briefly take in Harvey's own home at number 24. Walk down the footpath in between numbers 24 and 22 and turn left down Oak Tree Lane.

❺ You can extend your walk by just over half a mile (1 km) by turning right at Woodbrooke Road and walking a loop around Bournville Lake in Valley Parkway ★ . The Bournville Model Yachting Club has operated here since 1932 and you may catch a race on a Saturday morning. Back on Oak Tree Lane, pick up where you left off and continue down the road.

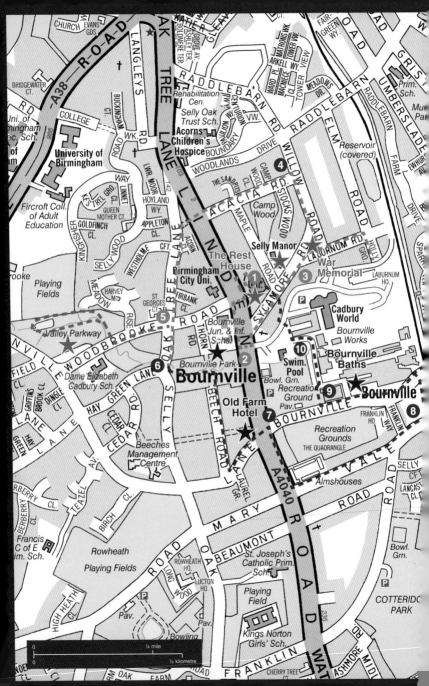

6 Turn left into Bournville Park ★ . Walk to the centre and turn right across Bourn Brook and up Beech Road to the end. Turn left onto Bournville Lane and walk down the snaking hill to rejoin Linden Road. On your left is Old Farm Hotel ★ which was originally a temperance inn, reflecting tee-totaller George Cadbury's aversion to alcohol, which was rooted in his Quakerism.

7 Turn right up Linden Road and take the first left onto Mary Vale Road. On your left are the almshouses established in 1987 by George's brother Richard Cadbury to house retired workers of the chocolate factory. You can spot his initials carved into the grand gatehouse. On your right are the 'Alphabet Houses', each with a place name on the colourful lintel above the front door. Walk down the road until you arrive at Bournville Station on your left. Walk under the purple archway and down the ramp.

8 Walk along the platform, down the stairs and out onto Bournville Lane. On the underside of the bridge on your right, you can see the repairs made after a bomb was dropped on the bridge in 1940. The street was flooded from the canal above. Turn away from the bridge so the station is on your left. Walk past the old Bournville Baths ★ on your right, taking in the memorial to the 218 Cadbury workers killed in the First World War.

9 As the timber-framed pavillion comes into view, turn right down the steps to the recreation ground. Walk past the Terpsichore statue by local sculptor William Bloye to commemorate the centenary of the Cadbury Factory in 1931. Walk down the ramp and through the factory grounds. Breathe deeply and smell the chocolate.

10 Walk alongside the imposing South Cocoa Block on your right. Cross over at the zebra crossing, turn right then follow the walkway as it bends to the left, away from the road. This will lead you to Sycamore Road. Cross at the zebra crossing, walk up the path and return to Bournville Village Green.

A–Z walk seventeen

The Village within the City

A tour of Old Yardley Village.

Over time, Birmingham city has encroached on and engulfed many old villages, such as Moseley and Harborne. However, nowhere in the city has retained its village atmosphere more than Old Yardley Village, which lies 6 miles (9.6 km) east of the city centre. Remarkably intact, Church Road does not feel like part of England's second city. For this reason, this time-capsule village was designated Birmingham's first conservation area in 1969 and is looked after by Yardley Conservation Society. Taking in the rural feel as you walk around, you get the impression that many locals would like to keep this secret hidden from the rest of the city.

This circular walk commences at the Tudor Blakesley Hall (1590), with its darkened timber and wattle-and-daub infill. Now a museum, you have the option to take a tour if it is open, before exploring Church Road where St Edburgha's Church sits in an ancient churchyard. Dating back to the 13th century, a secret gem can be found in the marks on the tower plinth, believed to be for sharpening arrowheads. After taking in the idyllic pedestrianized street, it's a circular route back to one of Birmingham's oldest buildings.

start / finish	Blakesley Hall Museum, Blakesley Road, Yardley
nearest postcode	B25 8RN
distance	1½ miles / 2.4 km
time	30 minutes (allow extra for visiting Blakesley Hall Museum)
terrain	Pavements and parkland, uneven cobbles on part of Church Road.

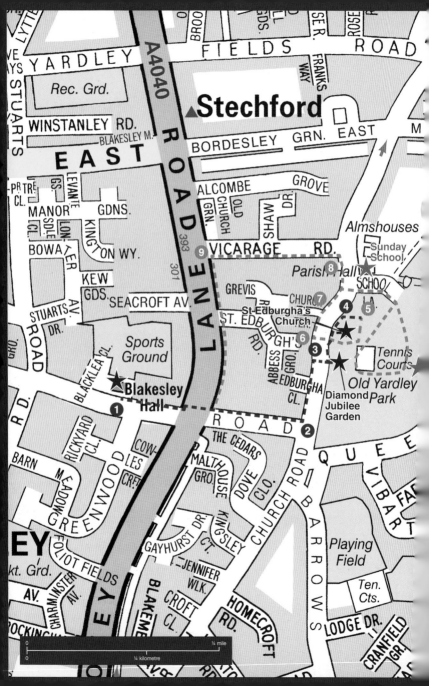

The walk starts at Blakesley Hall. There is a car park for visitors to the hall, alternatively there is on-street parking nearby.

❶ Blakesley Hall ★ was built by the Smalbroke family (who gave their name to the city road of Smallbrook Queensway) and the interior has been carefully restored to reflect the lifestyle of a wealthy Tudor and Stuart family. Look out for the Gilbertstone in the grounds, a volcanic rock which legend states was brought to Yardley by a giant named Gilbert. It's definitely worth taking a tour of the Hall, but check the opening times as they are limited and it closes over winter. Exit onto Blakesley Road and turn left. Walk down past the Homeleigh Hotel on your left. Cross over Stoney Lane and continue on Blakesley Road.

❷ At the end of Blakesley Road, turn left onto Church Road. On your right, across the road from St Edburgh's Road footpath is the beautiful Diamond Jubilee Garden ★ , which is definitely worth a quick walk around, especially if the roses are out. From the garden you can see the side of the timber-framed former Trust School built in the early 16th century.

❸ Return to Church Road. The building opposite (number 423–425) began life in 1710 as a cottage for local wheelwright, Thomas Roades. The small iron barred window is from the 1850's slaughterhouse and butcher's shop. Cross back over to the front of the School House to read the charming Yardley Parish Church noticeboard. Enter the path to St Edburgha's Church ★ . Named after an Anglo-Saxon princess, there has been a church on this site for over a thousand years. The church you see in front of you is an assembly of work from different centuries. On the plinth of the tower facing you are incisions thought to be for sharpening arrows.

❹ Walk in a clockwise direction around the church with its 147-foot (45-metre) tall spire, which dates from 1491 and was restored in 1898. On the north side of the church – almost opposite the porch on the south side – you can see 'Katherine's Door'. Look at the archway above the door and you can see carvings of a Tudor rose on the right and a pomegranate on the left. This celebrates the marriage of Catherine of Aragon to her first husband, Prince Arthur, who was King Henry VIII's older brother. A rare hidden bit of Tudor history in Birmingham!

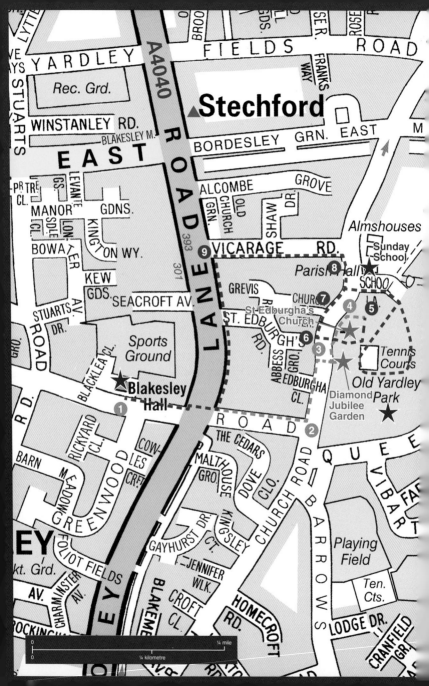

5 Continue walking around amid the mature trees of the churchyard and, at the far corner, you will see the lancet windows of the late 15th-century vestry. The chancel – the east-most part of the church – is the oldest and dates, incredibly, from the 13th century. On the south side of the chancel, behind gates in-between the chancel and the newer section, you can see the 13th-century priest's door for their direct access. Continuing going clockwise and you can see again the 15th-century porch which you should use to enter the church and check out its interior. Exit the church and return to Church Road.

6 Continue walking and pass the pebble-dashed cottage at number 431. You will now enter a pedestrianized section of the road with its paved and cobbled streets. Number 433 is a relatively modern meeting hall of 1882. Number 435 is a cute cottage built in 1826 for a local blacksmith.

7 Demonstrating that this industry still has a place in the 21st century, at number 453 is Collins Blacksmiths. This family-run business has been operating here since 1964. Turn right onto School Lane and walk to the end of the road. At this point, take the path on the right to do a short loop inside Old Yardley Park ★, returning to School Lane and retracing your steps to the end. Turn right onto Church Road.

8 Walk past the Sunday School ★ on the corner of School Lane and Church Road, and take the left turn onto Vicarage Road. Walk to the end of Vicarage Road and turn left onto Stoney Lane.

9 Walk down Stoney Lane on the path lined at either side with mature trees. Take the second turning on the right, back onto Blakesley Road, to return to the start.

ᴬZ walk eighteen

Medieval Meander

History and nature in the peaceful suburb of Kings Norton.

Just 6 miles (9.6 km) southwest of Birmingham city centre is the scenic ward of Kings Norton. This area has served as a settlement since Roman times and boasts an impressive display of historical significance. The once-chosen home of some seriously influential politicians such as Neville Chamberlain and Enoch Powell, as well as iconic performers such as Raymond Huntley (*Upstairs, Downstairs*) and Alan Napier (*Batman series*), the parish of Kings Norton remains a charming place to live. Much of its activity is based around The Green, including a monthly farmer's market and the 500-year-old tradition of The Mop Fair, held on the first Monday of October.

On this circular walk, you'll feel connected to nature as you follow the River Rea through Kings Norton Nature Reserve. The fairly quiet and unassuming setting of this area harbours some special hidden gems that still have cultural prevalence today. This is one of the city's finest residential areas, with the tranquil 17-acre (7-hectare) Merecroft Pool at the heart of it all on what was once the medieval estate belonging to Bordesley Abbey.

There are two possible starting points for this circular walk. Follow the directions from the beginning if you are arriving by bus or car, but if travelling by train, start at step 5.

start / finish	The Green, Kings Norton
nearest postcode	B38 8RS
distance	3½ miles / 5.5 km
time	1 hour 30 minutes
terrain	Pavements and muddy footpaths. Some steps.

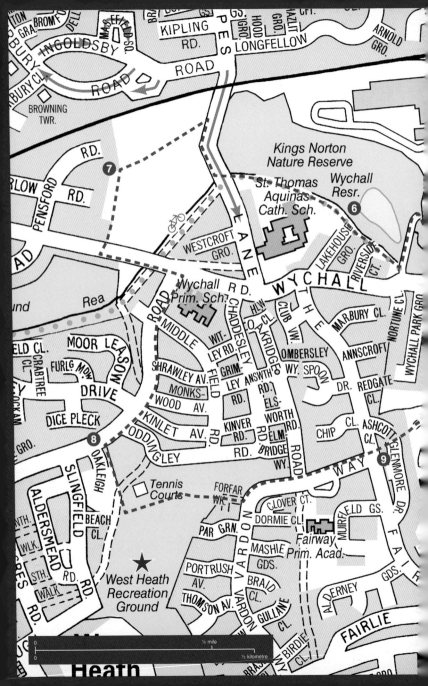

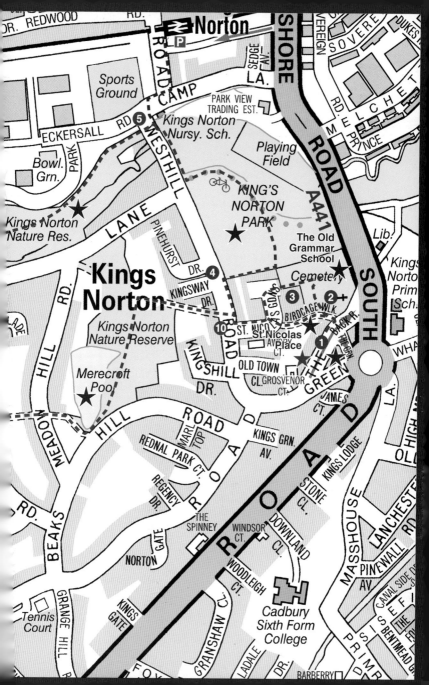

Buses from the city centre set down on the main A441 road, close to the village centre. Alternatively, on-street parking is available on The Green.

1 Begin this walk at The Green ★. With your back to the Bulls Head, turn left and head along the smaller Back Road and past St Nicolas Place ★ on your left. St Nicolas Place was built as a Tudor merchant's house in 1492 and in 1643, Queen Consort Henrietta Maria of England is reputed to have stayed here during the English Civil War. Although Central Birmingham itself supported the Parliamentarian Army (famously manufacturing 15,000 swords for them to wield), Kings Norton was a staunch Royalist ward and therefore a safe bet for resting Cavaliers and royalty. The black-and-white Saracen's Head on your left is supposedly haunted by the Queen's maid who caught influenza here and sadly died during this time. More recently, this group of buildings won the public vote on the BBC's *Restoration* programme in 2004.

2 Head through the entrance to the Parish Church. Although there has been a church on this site since the 11th century, the current church that you are looking at dates back to the 13th century. Reverend Wilbert Awdry took a curacy here for 6 years from 1940, in which time he created the characters of *Thomas the Tank Engine* to entertain his son who fell ill with measles in 1943. Follow the footpath around the church until you see the 15th-century black-and-white building

in the graveyard, which is now known as The Old Grammar School ★. In 1909, two women's suffragists broke into the school with the intention of burning it down in protest but were so charmed by its design that they left it intact (if a little graffitied with messages of equality). Continue until the footpath joins the tarmacked Miry Lane.

3 Continue on this lane through the gate and pass St Nicolas Rectory on your left. Carry on until the end of the lane then turn left onto St Nicolas Gardens. Go to the end of this road and then turn right to take the footpath. Continue along Westhill Road until you see some concrete steps to enter Kings Norton Park to the right. Head up here.

4 Enjoy a peaceful amble through Kings Norton Park ★, veering left at the first opportunity. You'll begin to follow the stream on your right as you head towards the northwest corner, keeping the play area on your left. Follow the footpath parallel to Westhill Road and then go over the bridge and to the end of the road. You'll see The Camp pub directly across the road from you, named so as it was the site where 5,500 Cavalier troops camped out during the English Civil War in the 17th century. To continue the walk from here, don't walk towards it, instead use the pedestrian crossing over Westhill Road and enter Kings Norton Nature Reserve ★. If you are returning to the train station, cross over to The Camp and walk up Station Road to the right of it.

5 (If you are starting the walk from the station, head down Station Road from the car park. Turn right into Camp Lane, cross Eckersall Road then immediately turn right into the Nature Reserve.) Follow the trail path along the River Rea for about 5 minutes and don't cross the river. This ribbon of nature reserve has been recognized since 2005 and is protected and looked after by the Friends of Kings Norton Nature Reserve. When you meet the Rea Valley Route lane, turn left onto it and then take the next right onto the footpath to continue your walk through the reserve. Keep an eye out for kingfishers, muntjac deer and woodpeckers.

6 Pass Wychall Reservoir on your right. Keep walking until you can cross a small footbridge and join Popes Lane. Turn right onto Popes Lane, continue for about 200 yards (180 metres) and then cross over to rejoin the trail through the metal fenced entrance. Follow the path directly through the middle of the nature reserve and turn left when you reach the perimeter.

7 Continue along this path until you emerge through the metal gated entrance onto Wychall Road. Turn left and go over the bridge, then take the next right onto Staple Lodge Road. Continue along Staple Lodge Road until you see the corner of another park – West Heath Park ★ . Take the path through the circular metal entrance.

8 Follow the path past the play area on your left. Turn left and continue past the play area and carry on straight until you cross a small bridge over the stream. Continue straight until you join a tarmacked lane named Forfar Walk and take the steps up to Vardon Way. Turn left onto Vardon Way and then carry on until it meets the T junction at The Fairway. Cross over onto the footpath directly opposite.

9 Continue on this path, crossing over Grassmoor Road and Meadow Hill Road. Once you are back on the footpath off Meadow Hill Road through the white railings/gates, continue until you have Merecroft Pool ★ on your left. Although part of the medieval Bordesley Abbey grounds, the lake you see today was dug as a late-Victorian boating lake. Continue to follow the path past Merecroft Pool to your left until you can turn right onto the footpath to exit the green space onto Westhill Road.

10 Turn right onto Westhill Road and then take the next left onto St Nicolas Gardens. Walk until the road starts to curve to the left and then take the footpath (Birdcage Walk) past the five terraced houses on your left. You should be able to see the church spire and be heading roughly towards it. Continue along Birdcage Walk until you emerge from behind St Nicolas Place and back onto The Green where you began this walk.

AZ walk nineteen

The Royal Town

Sutton Coldfield and Sutton Park.

Formerly in Warwickshire, the charming town of Sutton Coldfield became part of Birmingham and the new West Midlands metropolitan county in 1974. Lying 7½ miles (12 km) northeast of the city centre, its history dates back to the Bronze Age. It was also once favoured by King Henry VIII, who granted it royal town status in 1528, most likely at the request of his close friend Bishop John Vesey.

Part of this walk takes you to the wonderful Sutton Park, one of the largest urban parks in Europe. This former hunting forest was granted to the town in perpetuity by King Henry VIII but, today, it serves as the lungs of the town and neighbouring areas of Birmingham. Sutton Park covers more than 2,400 acres (9.7 square kilometres), most of which is a National Nature Reserve, and includes open heathland, woodlands, wetlands and lakes. Don't be surprised if you see the wild ponies that also graze on the land!

There are two possible starting points for this circular walk. Follow the directions from the beginning if you are arriving by car, but if travelling by train, start at step 5. There are facilities and refreshments available at Sutton Park, most easily accessible at the Town Gates entrance (step 6), to replenish you if you decide to venture further into the park.

start / finish	Boldmere Gate Car Park, Stonehouse Road
nearest postcode	B73 6LH
alternative start / finish	Sutton Coldfield Railway Station, Railway Road
nearest postcode	B73 6AY
distance	4 miles / 6.4 km
time	1 hour 30 minutes
terrain	Pavements and gravel/dirt footpaths. Moderate inclines.

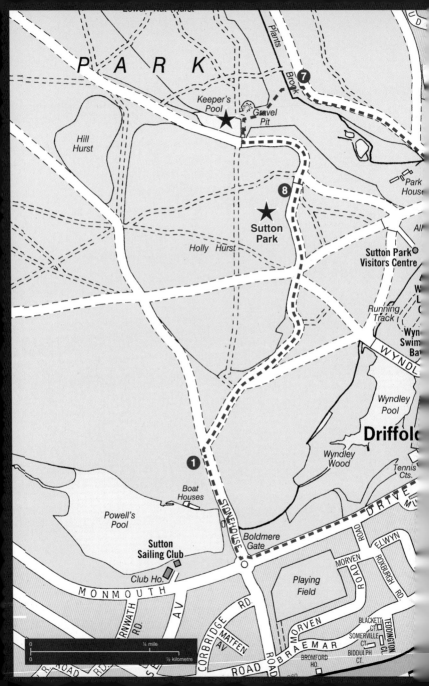

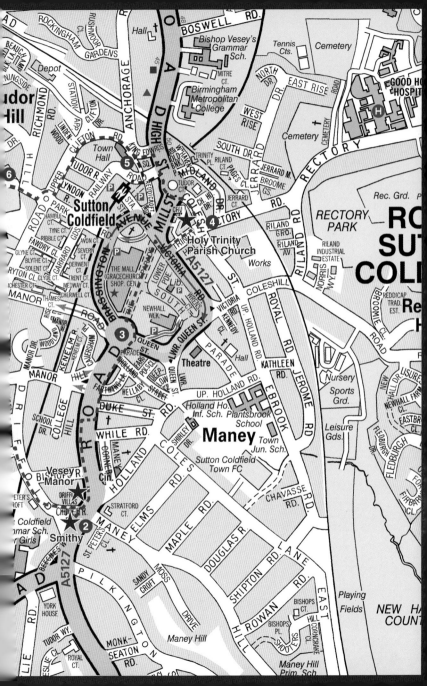

1 If starting the walk at Boldmere Gate car park, walk away from Sutton Park and down Stonehouse Road, with the lake on your right (you'll have chance to enjoy the park later!). Turn left onto Monmouth Drive and continue along, going straight over at the crossroads onto Digby Road. Continue down Digby Road and then turn right onto Driffold. Keep going until you can take the second left onto Church Road.

2 At the end of Church Road, go right and towards the traffic lights. You'll see Smithy ★ , a property which dates back to the 15th century, making it one of the oldest buildings in Sutton. Once you've had a peek at the now-art gallery, go back on yourself and cross over Church Road to keep going straight on Birmingham Road. On your left you'll see an example of the timber-framed Victorian Maney cottages, shortly followed by the 16th-century Vesey Manor ★ , originally built by Bishop John Vesey and now an antiques gallery. Continue along Birmingham Road, taking the opportunity to cross over it at the pedestrian crossing as you go.

3 At the roundabout, cross over Queen Street and continue onto The Parade, a pedestrianized shopping street. Keep to the left to stay on the pedestrianized area. At the end of this, follow the footpath down the slope to your right and cross over Lower Parade and then left over Victoria Road at the pedestrian crossing. Come back on yourself slightly to take the Trinity Hill road up past the right of the Baptist Church.

4 When you reach the top of Trinity Hill and a crossroads junction, turn left onto Coleshill Street. You will pass Holy Trinity Parish Church ★ on your left. Impressively, sections of the church have been here since the 13th century and the bell tower is also over 400 years old. Additionally, a lot of the residential properties here on Coleshill Street are Grade II listed. Keep going past the church on your left until the roundabout junction. Go straight over onto High Street. If you are finishing the walk at the railway station, take the first left up Railway Road, which will lead you to the station. Otherwise, continue along High Street and then take the left turn onto King Edward Square.

5 At the top of the road, you'll come upon the war memorial in the square, erected in 1922 and dedicated to the fallen soldiers of the First World War. (If you are starting the walk from the railway station, turn right out of the station then right again onto Railway Road. As you round the bend, look out for a path sloping up on the left at the end of the railings. This will lead you to King Edward Square, with the war memorial on your right.) The building to the left behind the memorial is the Town Hall, built originally as a hotel in 1865. After the completion of the extension in 1903, the clock tower you can see attached also served as a hose tower for the integrated fire headquarters. Head for this then continue past it, down Upper Clifton Road until you reach the roundabout. Turn right onto Park Road. Keep walking until you see the gated entrance to Sutton Park ★ on the corner.

6 Enter the park at Town Gate and then keep right as the footpath forks. You have the opportunity here to explore more of the park, but this walk provides a suggested short route. To follow this shorter route through the park, keep on this path going straight and past the turn for the carvery. At the next fork in the path, keep left. Keep left once again to take the footpath into the woodland. Once in the woodland, keep walking alongside the river on your left.

7 Take the first left, which should bring you over a footbridge. Continue on this footpath, ignoring the first left turn but taking the second left turn past Keeper's Pool ★ . This is one of many pools in Sutton Park built with the purpose of stocking fish. Keeper's Pool is actually one of the oldest, dating back to the Middle Ages. Once past Keeper's Pool, turn left and continue until you meet another fork in the road, then keep right.

8 Continue straight in this direction and on this path as far as possible (take the right-hand path when you meet a fork in the path) – you are heading towards the road, where you need to turn left onto it to get back to Boldmere Gate car park, where you began this walk.

AZ walk twenty

Escape to the Countryside

Lickey Hills and Barnt Green.

This is perhaps one of the best circular country walks within easy reach of Birmingham. The Lickey Hills Country Park is a 524-acre (2-square kilometre) park featuring staggering views over the city, towering coniferous trees and carpets of bluebells in spring. The philanthropic Birmingham Society for the Preservation of Open Spaces gradually purchased the woods and hills on behalf of the city from 1888 onwards. With the tram track that extended down Bristol Road to Rednal increasing accessibility, the hills became incredibly popular, with 20,000 visitors recorded on the August Bank Holiday of 1919!

Starting at the country park's Visitor Centre, 11 miles (17.7 km) southwest of the city centre, this walk takes you through the Lickey Hills, across Cofton Hackett and along waterways to Barnt Green before returning through Pinfields Wood.

Since the route passes by Barnt Green Railway Station, there is an option to arrive by train and start the walk from step 9 instead.

start / finish	Lickey Hills Visitor Centre, Warren Lane, Cofton Hackett
nearest postcode	B45 8ER
distance	5 miles / 8 km
time	2 hours
terrain	Pavements and paths, which can be muddy. Hills and steps to climb and descend. Turnstiles.

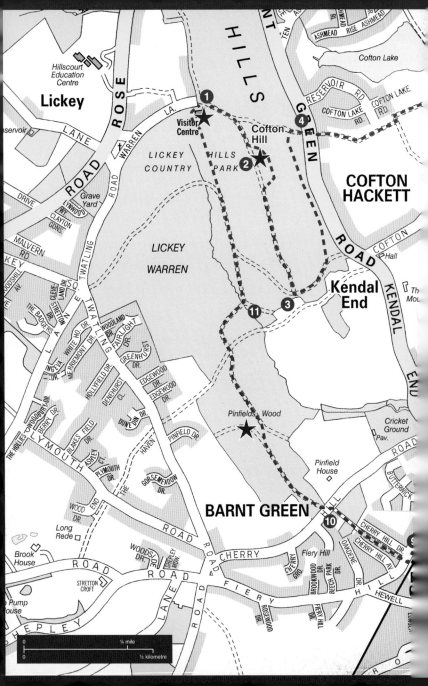

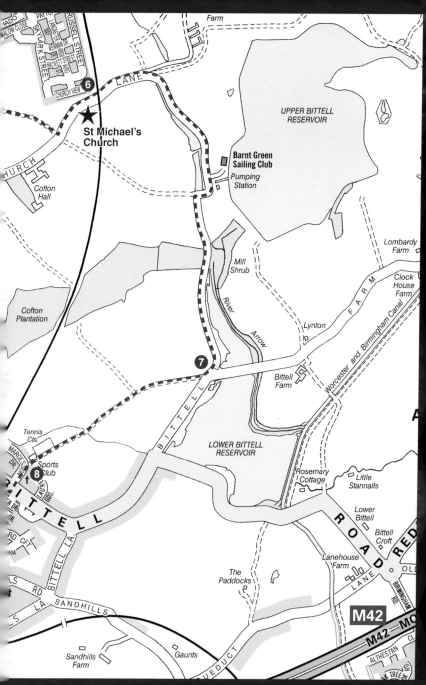

Parking is available at the Lickey Hills Visitor Centre car park. If you wish to travel by train, there is a regular service between Birmingham New Street and Barnt Green, from where you can start the walk at step 9, being sure to emerge from the station onto Fiery Hill Road, beside platform 1.

1 Facing the Visitor Centre ★, take the path to the right of it and walk up the steps on the right. Walk along the path on the grass, with the car park on your left. Join the main path and follow it up to Cofton Hill ★. You'll arrive at an open area with a distant view over the whole of Birmingham city. Clearly identifiable buildings are the Old Joe Clocktower, Queen Elizabeth Hospital and the BT Tower.

2 Rejoin the path you were on and walk down the hill into the forest area. Be careful after rain as this path can get a bit muddy. Follow this path downhill for about a third of a mile (0.5 km) amid the pine and fir trees. Eventually this will terminate at a path going across.

3 Take the left path, which follows the road uphill. After about another third of a mile (0.5 km) there will be a path leading down towards the road on your right. Take this path, which is the most uneven on the walk so be careful with your steps. This will lead you down to the road.

4 Being very careful, cross over Barnt Green Road and walk down the tarmacked road opposite, which has fences on either side. This may feel like a private drive but it is a public footpath. Follow this down the hill and a footpath will lead out onto Cofton Hackett. This arable field has beautiful views south towards Barnt Green, especially on a sunny day. Walk along the footpath on the left of the field. You will come to a kissing gate leading onto a very narrow road.

5 Cross directly over and into the next field. Follow the footpath down and as it bends towards the right. In spring, wild flowers grow in the hedgerow to your left. Walk through the kissing gate and turn left onto Cofton Church Lane. After 165 yards (150 metres) you will see St Michael's Church ★ on your right. This red sandstone church largely dates back to the 14th century and was restored in 1861. It's usually locked but you may be lucky! In the churchyard are two listed monuments. One a square stone base that used to hold a cross dating to the 15th century. The other is the tomb of Thomas Green surrounded by railings.

6 Return to Cofton Church Lane and follow it under the rail bridge. Continue down the road as it forks to the right. Follow this down with the fishing pond on your right. Occasionally swans can be seen nesting here. Keep going past the sailing club and eventually you will be walking alongside a stream to your right.

7 You will emerge onto Bittell Farm Road. Take the footpath immediately on your right. Walk diagonally over the field. The footpath will lead you over the right side of the second field. Continue along the path, through the gate and you will emerge into a small public park. Continue along the footpath and take the first turn on your right which will lead you out behind the sports centre.

8 Turn left on Margesson Drive, walk to the end and turn right onto Bittell Road. Take the second left onto Hewell Road, at the mini-roundabout. The road takes you into Barnt Green, which has a nice selection of independent shops that you may wish to explore. At the shops, take the right turn onto Station Approach. Follow the road to the left and use the footbridge to cross over the Cross City Line at Barnt Green Station.

9 Cross over Fiery Hill Road and enter the path behind the wooden gate, to the left of Cherry Hill Drive. Walk up this attractive tree-lined path to the end, where it emerges onto Cherry Hill Road.

10 Cross over the road and enter the Lickey Hills Country Park again through the gate to the left. The Visitor Centre is a one-mile (1.6-km) walk from here. Follow the path all the way up through Pinfields Wood ★. In the spring this area is usually covered in bluebells. This path will curve to the right and you will walk downhill slightly, crossing over the stream.

11 Follow the path around to the left and continue in a relatively straight line going uphill all the way to the Visitor Centre.

images